D1321256

Chapman's
Car Compendium

Chapman's Car Compendium

The Essential Book of Car Facts and Trivia

Giles Chapman

MERRELL

LONDON · NEW YORK

Introduction

One day in March 1995 remains etched on my mind. I had journeyed to Basle in Switzerland to interview the country's most successful (and just about only) car tycoon. A short, dapper, intense figure, Peter Monteverdi had decided to stop manufacturing cars, and had instead turned his factory into a museum – dedicated to himself.

There was one of every type of car that Monteverdi had built, most of which I had only ever seen in grainy photographs, together with numerous other models that he owned from such exotic manufacturers as Porsche and Ferrari. The cars were arranged in tightly packed displays in an entirely underground complex, with the walls painted a lurid apple-green and thick carpets in deep crimson.

As if the surroundings were not oppressive enough, during the interview one of the employees accidentally threw the power switch, and the whole place was plunged into darkness. Mr Monteverdi, whose answers to my questions had been on the ripe side of frank, fairly erupted in fury.

Monteverdi's claim that this was Switzerland's biggest car museum may well have been true, but I was the only visitor, and the receptionist at the downtown hotel where I was staying had never heard of it. Of course, it all made delicious material for a magazine profile. Rather sadly, it also provided the insight I needed to write Mr Monteverdi's obituary three years later for a national newspaper. Most of all, however, and despite my having a lifelong fascination with cars, it had all been totally unexpected. As a reporter and a recorder, that's what you dearly hope for but so rarely get. That's why the chance to write this book was so utterly irresistible. It's the opportunity to bring together all the unexpected bits – and so very much more – from a 25-year career of trying to unearth interesting stuff about cars.

There are lists, anecdotes, league tables and trivia; things that have made me laugh and other issues that I've found galling. Some of it you could, conceivably, discover online, but *Chapman's Car Compendium* is a book where the surfing and sifting has been done for you, and all you have to do is dip in at will, or dart around randomly through the facts, feats and figures. Or else read the whole lot cover to cover. Enjoy it, because I've enjoyed assembling it all.

Like Peter Monteverdi, I'm a bit of a complete-ist myself – someone who likes to have the details in order. Unlike him, however, I've never actually contributed so much as a hubcap to the three-dimensional, big wide world of the car. I hope you feel that *Chapman's Car Compendium* does that world justice.

'An invisible car came out of nowhere, struck my car and vanished.'

———————————

'Q: Could either driver have done anything to avoid the accident?

A: Travelled by bus.'

Car insurance claims

The pace of the horsepower race quickens

Between 2003 and 2007 the league table of the most powerful production cars of all time received an unprecedented boost. The output of the available models took an extraordinary leap, with the most powerful of all increasing by more than the equivalent of the entire brake horsepower of a Porsche 911 Carrera 3.8 (350 bhp).

This was the Top 10 league in 2003:

1. **Ferrari Enzo**
   660 bhp

2. **McLaren F1 LM**
   659 bhp

3. **Koenigsegg CC 8S**
   655 bhp

4. **Mercedes-Benz SLR McLaren**
   617 bhp

5. **Bugatti EB110SS**
   611 bhp

6. **Porsche Carrera GT**
   603 bhp

7. **Aston Martin Vantage Le Mans/Vector W8** 600 bhp

8. **Lamborghini Diablo E30 Jota**
   590 bhp

9. **Lamborghini Murcielago**
   571 bhp

10. **Bentley Continental GT**
    552 bhp

And this was the same league just four years later:

1. **Bristol Fighter T**
   1012 bhp

2. **Bugatti Veyron** *Illustrated below*
   987 bhp

3. **SSC Aero SC/8T**
   908 bhp

4. **Koenigsegg CCR and CCX**
   806 bhp

5. **Saleen S7 Twin-Turbo**
   750 bhp

6. **Ferrari Enzo/Bristol Fighter S**
   660 bhp

7. **McLaren F1 LM**
   659 bhp

8. **Koenigsegg CC 8S**
   655 bhp

9. **Maserati MC12**
   632 bhp

10. **Mercedes-Benz SLR McLaren**
    617 bhp

The two-year calendar for major motor shows

All motor shows are a spectacle, and great fun, but these are where you'll find all the important new cars making their debuts:

CHINA	Beijing Auto Show, June biennially in even years
FRANCE	Paris Motor Show, September/October biennially in even years
GERMANY	Frankfurt Motor Show, September biennially in odd years
ITALY	Bologna Motor Show, December annually
JAPAN	Tokyo Motor Show, October/November biennially in odd years
SOUTH KOREA	Seoul Motor Show, March/April biennially in odd years
SWITZERLAND	Geneva Motor Show, March annually
UK	London Motor Show, July biennially in even years
USA	North American Auto Show, Detroit, January annually
USA	New York International Motor Show, March/April annually
USA	Greater Los Angeles Auto Show, December annually

Lost property in London cabs

If you leave something in a London taxi it may well end up at the Transport for London Lost Property Office on Baker Street. The office is one of the world's biggest, handling about 130,000 items a year, including lost property found on trains, buses and the London Underground. In the latest year for which statistics are available (April 2003–March 2004), the office received the following items:

24,084	cases and bags
20,846	books (including diaries and chequebooks)
19,583	items of clothing
14,112	'value' items, such as wallets and purses
10,614	mobile phones
7505	sets of keys
7026	umbrellas
6118	pairs of glasses
2671	pairs of gloves and 474 single gloves
803	perishable items, including food

Who owns what in the car industry?

From literally hundreds of separate companies, the automotive industry has today consolidated into 13 carmaking groups. They are: BMW, Daimler-Benz, Chrysler, Fiat, Ford, General Motors, Honda, Hyundai, Peugeot, Renault, Suzuki, Toyota and Volkswagen. But of the several dozen marques currently on sale in developed markets, who owns (or else, controls) what? This guide should help.

BMW	BMW, Mini and Rolls-Royce
Daimler-Benz*	Maybach, Mercedes-Benz and Smart
Chrysler	Chrysler, Dodge and Jeep
Fiat	Alfa Romeo, Ferrari, Fiat, Lancia and Maserati
Ford	Daimler, Ford, Jaguar, Land Rover, Lincoln, Mazda, Mercury and Volvo
General Motors	Buick, Cadillac, Chevrolet, GMC, Holden, Hummer, Opel, Pontiac, Saab, Saturn and Vauxhall
Honda	Acura and Honda
Hyundai	Hyundai and Kia
Peugeot	Citroën and Peugeot
Renault	Dacia, Infiniti, Nissan, Renault and Samsung
Suzuki	Suzuki
Toyota	Daihatsu, Lexus, Scion, Subaru and Toyota
Volkswagen	Audi, Bentley, Bugatti, Lamborghini, Seat, Skoda and Volkswagen

* anticipated title at the time of going to press

Significant 'independents' making their own designs of car include Germany's Porsche, India's Tata, Japan's Mitsubishi, Malaysia's Proton/Lotus and Russia's VAZ (Lada). Chinese manufacturers tipped for possible inclusion shortly in this group include Chery, China Brilliance (makers of ZhongHua cars), Geely, Nanjing and Shanghai Automotive (owner of South Korea's SsangYong).

The name in Spain ... is mostly on the boot lid

There's something curiously alluring about the names of Spanish towns and cities, and they have become a favourite with carmakers when it comes to naming their products:

Cordoba	Between 1975 and 1983 this was the sonorous name of Chrysler's 'personal luxury' car in North America, and was later used by Seat too (1993).
Granada	Adopted by Ford in 1972 for its executive range; the name lasted 23 years, surviving a lawsuit from Granada Television.
Ibiza	Off to the Balearics for Seat in 1984, using the name of a holiday hotspot for its Ford Fiesta rival.
Leon	Just inland of Spain's northern coast, this city, famous for its cathedral, was immortalized as a Seat in 1999.
Malaga	While Ronda was the badge on Seat's five-door hatchback, this followed on the four-door saloon version in 1985.
Marbella	Warming to the theme, three years later, Seat plumped for another sun-kissed resort for its Fiat Panda-based city car.
Ronda	A town near Spain's southern tip, this was the first conurbation used by Seat in its naming strategy, in 1982.
Seville	Chosen by Cadillac in 1975, and survives to this day. Cadillac also first used 'Eldorado' in 1953, saluting the imaginary 'golden' city.
Toledo	First honoured by Triumph in 1970 for its smallest saloon, the name is now used by Seat on its largest one.

The 10 longest road tunnels

Without these enormous tubes buried deep underground, the motoring world would be a smaller, more restricted place:

Lærdal, Norway 24.5 km (15¼ miles) – opened November 2000

Zhongnanshan, China 18.04 km (11⅛ miles) – opened January 2007

Gotthard, Switzerland 16.9 km (10½ miles) – opened September 1980

Arlberg, Austria 13.9 km (8¾ miles) – opened December 1978

Hsuehshan, Taiwan 12.9 km (8 miles) – opened June 2006

Fréjus, France/Italy 12.8 km (8⅛ miles) – opened July 1980

Mont Blanc/Monte Bianco, France/Italy 11.6 km (7¼ miles) – opened July 1965

Gudvanga, Norway 11.4 km (7⅛ miles) – opened December 1991

Folgefonn, Norway 11.1 km (6¼ miles) – opened June 2001

Kan-etsu, Japan (south-bound tube) 11 km (6¼ miles) – opened 1991

Cars named specially for the US market

The US car market is the world's largest and most competitive, and foreign manufacturers often change their products' names to be more attractive to the critical American buyer. Here are some of those Stateside titles, and their original ones:

Marque	USA	Most other places
Audi	5000	100
Austin	America	1300
Fiat	Strada	Ritmo
Isuzu	Impulse	Piazza
Isuzu	Rodeo	MU
Jaguar	XKE	E-type
Lancia	Scorpion	Monte Carlo
Lancia	Zagato	Beta Spider
Mazda	Protegé	Familia
Mitsubishi	Montero	Pajero
Renault	Alliance	9
Renault	Encore	11
Renault	Le Car	5
Suzuki	Sidekick	Vitara
Volkswagen	Dasher	Passat
Volkswagen	Rabbit	Golf Mk1
Volkswagen	The Thing	181

These five cars underwent an entire identity change to appeal to US buyers:

USA	Most other places
Cadillac Catera	Opel Omega
Jaguar Vanden Plas	Daimler Double-Six
Merkur XR4i	Ford Sierra XR4i
Plymouth Cricket	Hillman Avenger
Sterling	Rover 800

The mysterious code of wheels and tyres

The basic size and type of wheels and tyres are always embossed on a tyre wall in an internationally accepted formula. Representative examples include 315/70R17, 235/50VR18, 225/50WR17 and 225/40ZR18. In all cases, the first number before the slash is the tyre width in millimetres. The number after the slash is the height-to-width 'aspect' ratio of the tyre section expressed as a percentage. The letter R denotes radial construction (crossply tyres are still produced, but not for cars). Letters preceding R indicate the tyre's speed rating and denote the maximum safe operating speed, as follows:

N	140 KM/H (87 MPH)	T	190 KM/H (118 MPH)
P	150 KM/H (93 MPH)	H	210 KM/H (130 MPH)
Q	160 KM/H (99 MPH)	V/Z	240 KM/H (149 MPH)
R	170 KM/H (106 MPH)	W	270 KM/H (168 MPH)
S	180 KM/H (112 MPH)	Y	300 KM/H (186 MPH)

The number after the letter R is the diameter of the wheel in inches. An additional numerical code, ranging from 65 to 119, indicates the weight that the tyre can support at maximum speed: 65 is 290 kilograms (640 lb), and 119 is 1360 kilograms (3000 lb).

The bestselling single models ever

These are the all-time bestselling single car designs – and therefore the bestselling cars of all time. There is no Toyota Corolla here, of which more than 30 million examples have been sold. That's because there have been nine entirely different Corolla cars. However, the Corolla nameplate is still the most successful ever.

1 Volkswagen Beetle

Sitting at the top, and destined always to be there, forever and ever, amen. Just to recap: 21,529,464 sold between 1939 and 2003. *Illustrated opposite.*

2 Fiat 124/Lada (VAZ 2101-2107)

Including some 2.9 million Seat (Spanish), Tofas (Turkish) and Premier (Indian) cars, 15,400,000 examples have been sold since the Fiat was introduced in 1966 (Lada in 1970). And, thanks to its unique suitability to the Russian roadscape, 200,000 still sell annually.

3 Ford Model T

Until 17 February 1972, when the Beetle edged ahead, this was the bestselling single car design, with 15,007,033 sold between 1908 and 1927. All black, all tinny, all over the place. *Illustrated opposite.*

4 Fiat Uno

Brazil is the last remaining source for brand-new Fiat Unos. But what an achievement: introduced in 1983 and, 8,500,000-plus cars later, still on sale!

5 Renault 4

Gestures triumphantly at the car that inspired it, the Citroën 2CV, of which 'just' 5,114,267 were sold: there were 8,135,422 takers for the 4 between its 1961 debut and its 1993 demise.

6 Volkswagen Golf Mk1

Introduced in 1974 and still built in South Africa (where it wears the name of City Golf and is the surest way out of the townships). Total output is nudging 6.9 million.

7 Volkswagen Golf Mk2

By contrast with the early Renault 5, this car, made between 1983 and 1991, seemingly lasts eternally. VW's factories worldwide, as well as in Germany, stamped out 6,300,987.

8 Peugeot 206

One of three cars in the Top 10 still available new. By the end of December 2006, 5,644,749 had been sold. And still they pour out, in Argentina, Brazil, France and Iran.

9 Renault 5 Mk1

By rights, it should be omnipresent, because Renault made 5,471,701 between 1972 and 1983, but rust has rendered it probably the world's leading motoring landfill.

10 BMC/British Leyland/Rover Mini

This revolutionary little car had a very long life, with 5,387,862 sold between 1959 and 2000, even though it's said to have taken many years to make a profit; it beats the Peugeot 205 (5,278,050 sold between 1983 and 1998) into eleventh place.

Bumper stickers

These legends have supposedly all been spotted adorning the otherwise cheerless tail-ends of cars and trucks across the United States.

IF you can read this, I've lost the trailer!

Corduroy pillows: they're making headlines!

I'M IN NO HURRY. I'M ON MY WAY TO WORK.

September 12: Sell Your SUV Day!

You never see a Harley parked in front of a shrink's office.

IF YOU DON'T LIKE THE WAY I'M DRIVING, YOU COME AND GET THESE HANDCUFFS OFF.

IF YOU CAN READ THIS, PLEASE FLIP ME BACK OVER.

[seen upside-down, on a Jeep]

Alcohol and calculus don't mix. Never drink and derive.

MY OTHER CAR!

I want to die peacefully in my sleep like my grandfather ... not screaming and yelling like the passengers in his car.

Jesus Saves ... He passes it to Gretzky ... Gretzky shoots ... He scores!

How do they get the deer to cross at that yellow road sign?

I brake *for no apparent reason.*

Eat right. Exercise. Die anyway.

Don't laugh! Your daughter could be in this vehicle.

The speediest drop-tops

In 2003 journalists at Britain's *Auto Express* magazine had a bit of time on their hands, so they thought they'd play with the buttons and discover which convertible had the most rapid electric roof mechanism. This was the result:

Honda S2000	6 seconds
Audi TT roadster	9 seconds
BMW Z4	10 seconds
VW Beetle cabriolet	13 seconds
Mercedes-Benz SLK *Illustrated below*	15 seconds
Citroën C3 Pluriel	16 seconds
Ferrari 360 Spider	19 seconds
Mercedes-Benz CLK cabriolet	20 seconds
Saab 9-3 convertible	20 seconds
Renault Mégane Coupé Cabriolet	22 seconds

Cars in pop and rock music titles

The roaring engine, the pounding of tyres on tarmac, the magic of a slinky roadster – these are all things that have inspired singers and songwriters to make cars an integral part of popular music.

These 10 top tracks salute cars and driving in general:

Autobahn by Kraftwerk, 1974

Cars by Gary Numan, 1979

Cars and Girls by Prefab Sprout, 1988

Drive by The Cars, 1984

Drive My Car by The Beatles, 1965

Driving Home for Christmas by Chris Rea, 1988

Driving in My Car by Madness, 1982

Fast Car by Tracy Chapman, 1988

The Passenger by Iggy Pop, 1977

Ullo John! Got a New Motor? by Alexei Sayle, 1982

Here are 10 more tracks that, more unusually, name a specific car:

2CV by Lloyd Cole and the Commotions, 1984

Austin Ambassador Y-Reg by John Shuttleworth (Graham Fellows), 1996

Jaguar by The Who, 1967

Little Deuce Coupe by The Beach Boys, 1963

Little GTO by Ronny and the Daytonas, 1964

Little Red Corvette by Prince, 1983

Mercedes-Benz by Janis Joplin, 1971

MGB GT by Richard Thompson, 1994

Mustang Sally by Wilson Pickett, 1966

Pink Cadillac by Bruce Springsteen, 1988 (but a bigger hit for Natalie Cole)

Design inspirations

In 1999 London's Royal College of Art (RCA) asked five of its influential car-design graduates – by then high-flying designers in the car industry itself – what non-automotive objects they used as reference points. This was their response:

Tony Hatter, designer, Porsche AG, Stuttgart, Germany. Graduated 1981

'I just love machines. Watches, or John Harrison's wooden maritime timepieces. Or an old machine shop where the lathes are driven from a central power source by leather belts. It's all fascinating to me.'

Keith Helfet, principal designer, advanced projects, Jaguar Cars, Coventry, UK. Graduated 1977

'Along with many other designers and artists, my point of reference is the human body. In particular, the female body has form that can be functional, beautiful and sensual – that combination of pure function with desire is, for me, an inspiration and the true challenge of design.'

Graham Hull, chief stylist, Rolls-Royce and Bentley Motor Cars,

Crewe, UK. Graduated 1971

'I tend to like design at the extremes where compromise is minimal – aircraft are great for this, and boats. A racing bicycle is an icon of design beauty. Any tightly focused design brief inevitably leads to a convincing solution.'

Pinky Lai, design manager, Porsche AG, Stuttgart, Germany. Graduated 1980

'Basketball shoes, running shoes, ski boots and sports gear have a very strong emotional and design impact on me. Occasionally, architecture makes me feel lost in an unknown time and dimension – the Guggenheim Museum in Bilbao took my breath away, instantly.'

Giles Taylor, principal stylist, Jaguar Cars, Coventry, UK. Graduated 1992

'Architecture: Frank Lloyd Wright interiors, New York's Chrysler Building, Lord's Pavilion. Watches. Military design – engineering for function. I own an ex-RAF lightweight Land Rover for its thorough honesty of form.'

Cars styled by Italians

Ever since the 1940s, Italy has been a centre of car styling, its resident designers employed by carmakers all over the world to bestow visual sophistication and product kudos. The trouble is, those clients don't always like to reveal where they get such style, which is why we spill some beans here:

BMW 1500	**GERMANY, 1961** by Michelotti
Citroën BX	**FRANCE, 1982** by Bertone
Daewoo Lanos	**SOUTH KOREA, 1997** by Italdesign/Giugiaro
Daewoo Tacuma	**SOUTH KOREA, 2000** by Pininfarina
Daf 44	**THE NETHERLANDS, 1965** by Michelotti
Ford Streetka	**EUROPE, 2003** by Ghia
Hafei Saibao	**CHINA, 2005** by Pininfarina
Hyundai Matrix	**SOUTH KOREA, 2001** by Pininfarina
Hyundai Stellar	**SOUTH KOREA, 1983** by Italdesign/Giugiaro *Illustrated below*
Reliant Scimitar SS1	**UK, 1984** by Michelotti
Renault 21	**FRANCE, 1986** by Italdesign/Giugiaro
Rolls-Royce Camargue	**UK, 1975** by Pininfarina
Seat Toledo	**SPAIN, 1991** by Italdesign/Giugiaro
Skoda Favorit	**CZECHOSLOVAKIA, NOW CZECH REPUBLIC, 1987** by Bertone
Suzuki SX4	**JAPAN, 2006** by Italdesign/Giugiaro
Volkswagen Polo	**GERMANY, 1975** by Bertone
Volvo P1800	**SWEDEN, 1961** by Frua
Yugo Sana	**YUGOSLAVIA, NOW SERBIA, 1988** by Italdesign/Giugiaro

Car manufacturing in … Scotland

Scotland is noted for many things, but making cars is not one of them. While singularly lacking in car companies today, however, it has a surprisingly rich automotive heritage, as these highlights demonstrate.

Argyll 25/50 hp (1913)

This large four-cylinder machine helped make Glasgow-based Argyll Motors Britain's fifth-biggest carmaker by 1914, although that year it went bust after building a vast, marble-lined factory that today is a shopping centre.

Beardmore 15 hp taxi (1919)

Only one in every dozen Beardmores sold was a private car. Cabbies across Britain latched on to the rugged, purpose-built taxi model, even though heavy steering made it tiring to drive.

Rob Roy 8 hp (1922)

Sounds like a hire car for American tourists, but this was actually a kind of Scottish Austin Seven, built in Glasgow with a two-cylinder engine under its attractive bonnet. The manufacturer was bankrupt by 1924.

Albion Shooting Brake (1927)

Another Glasgow enterprise, in Scotstoun, Albion started making cars in 1899. Well-heeled customers instead latched on to its truck-based shooting brake (*illustrated below*), ideal for transporting shooting parties over Highland estates.

Hillman Imp (1963)

A huge plant near Glasgow made this boxy, rear-engined answer to the Mini. Some 440,000 were sold up to 1976, including Singer, Sunbeam and Commer editions.

Scamp (1967)

This was an attempt by Scottish Aviation of Prestwick to design an electric shopping car. Britain's Electricity Board was keen to sell the car through its 2000 showrooms ... until reports of unsafe prototypes scuppered the plan.

Talbot Sunbeam (1979)

On 1977 TV ads, singer Petula Clark urged viewers to 'Put a Chrysler Sunbeam in your life', as the Linwood-built successor to the Imp was launched. Many did; then the car became a Talbot two years later.

AC ME3000 (1984)

This mid-engined sports car moved from Surrey to Hillington, Glasgow, in 1984 after AC sold up to a Scottish businessman. He sold only 30 more cars on top of the ME3000's pathetic 1979–83 tally of 68 before closing down.

Argyll Turbospeed (1984)

Revealed eight years before it went on sale, this revival of the Argyll name was by Scottish engineer Bob Henderson. It had a turbocharged Renault V6 engine but looked ungainly, and few were sold.

Haldane MkII (1991)

This fairly accurate replica of the Austin-Healey 100 began as a 1987 one-off but was offered as a kit car in 1991, to which the DIY mechanic could add a Ford or Toyota engine.

10 fast-car towns

To car enthusiasts, certain places are motoring meccas, synonymous with specific marques; to others, however, it may come as a surprise that these far-flung outposts have any motoring connections at all.

Blackpool, UK	Lancashire seaside resort famous, until 2006, for TVR sports cars, in which a kiss-me-very-quick hat is a must.
Bowling Green, USA	This city in small-town Kentucky is the home of the great all-American sports car, the Chevrolet Corvette.
Coventry, UK	The Luftwaffe flattened its cathedral, but nothing could destroy the spirit of the home of Jaguar.
Crewe, UK	It rains a lot in Cheshire; that doesn't take the shine off the town where Bentleys have been made for 60 years.
Ingolstadt, Germany	Not really on the tourist trail, but this is the place where Audi's lateral thinkers came up with the quattro concept.
Modena, Italy	Centre of the supercar universe, with famous residents including Ferrari, Maserati, De Tomaso and Pagani.
Newport Pagnell, UK	Get beyond the nearby M1 motorway and you'll find a charming Buckinghamshire town where Aston Martins rule the streets.
Norwich, UK	Aha! Alan Partridge isn't the only famous export from rural Norfolk; there's also a galaxy of Lotus sports cars.
Stuttgart, Germany	Once the site of a solitary stud farm; now horses are part of Porsche's famous badge, which is essentially the city's coat of arms.
Tochigi, Japan	Since both the Honda NS-X and Nissan Skyline GT-R hail from here, in the centre of Honshu island, this must be some sort of fast-car temple in Japan.

National racing colours

A system of distinguishing competition cars from one another with different-coloured paintwork was instigated in 1900 for the Gordon Bennett Trophy race, one of the very first motor-sport events. Even after this race series finished in 1905, the system persisted, with Egypt one of the last to join it in 1956. Ten years on, it had mostly been replaced by sponsorship, with only Italy's Ferraris sticking with the colours system today.

Country	Paintwork	Racing numbers
ARGENTINA	Blue; yellow bonnet	Red-on-white
AUSTRALIA	Green; gold bonnet	Blue
AUSTRIA	Blue	Black-on-white
BELGIUM	Yellow	Black
BRAZIL	Pale yellow; green wheels	Black
BULGARIA	Green; white bonnet	Red-on-white
CANADA	Red; white stripes (originally white; green stripes)	Black
CHILE	Red/white; blue bonnet	Blue- or red-on-white
CUBA	Yellow; black bonnet	Black
CZECHOSLOVAKIA	White/red; white/blue bonnet	Blue
DENMARK	Grey; Danish flag on bonnet	Red-on-white
EGYPT	Purple	Red-on-white
FINLAND	White; blue cross on bonnet	Black-on-white
FRANCE	Blue	White
GERMANY	Silver (originally white)	Red
GREAT BRITAIN	Green	White
GREECE	Pale blue; white bonnet stripes	Black-on-white
HUNGARY	White/green; red bonnet	Black
IRELAND	Green; orange stripes	White
ITALY	Red (originally black)	White
JAPAN	White; red circle on bonnet	Black
JORDAN	Brown	Black-on-white
LUXEMBOURG	Red; white-and-blue stripes	Black-on-white
MEXICO	Gold; blue bonnet stripe	Red-on-white
MONACO	Gold; blue bonnet stripe	Black-on-white
THE NETHERLANDS	Orange	White
POLAND	White/red	Red-on-white
PORTUGAL	Red/white	White
SOUTH AFRICA	Gold; green bonnet	Black-on-yellow
SPAIN	Red; yellow bonnet	Black-on-yellow/white-on-red
SWEDEN	Blue/yellow; three blue bonnet stripes	White
SWITZERLAND	Red; white bonnet	Black
THAILAND	Pale blue; yellow band and wheels	White-on-blue
URUGUAY	Pale blue; red bonnet band	White-on-black
USA	Blue and white (originally red)	Blue-on-white

The 10 most expensive production cars

(1) **Mercedes-Benz CLK LM**
£957,000
1999

(2) **Bugatti Veyron**
£840,000
2005

(3) **McLaren F1 LM**
£680,000
1995

(4) **Porsche 911 GT1 Road**
c. **£570,000**
1998

(5) **Maserati MC12**
£515,000
2004

(6) **Pagani Zonda F Roadster**
c. **£450,000**
2006

(7) **Ferrari Enzo** *Illustrated below*
£425,000
2002

(8) **Jaguar XJ220**
£403,000
1992

(9) **Koenigsegg CCX**
£370,000
2006

(10) **Koenigsegg 8C SS**
£354,500
2003

Acronyms on road vehicles worldwide

Some car and vehicle names don't bear repetition on the products themselves; they're too wordy, too corporate or too obscure to be used in full. So snappy shortenings were adopted early on as a means of identification. This thorough list includes most of those that you are likely to encounter on the world's roads, together with a guide to what they are found adorning.

Acronym	Stands for	Vehicle(s)
AC	Auto Carriers	Cars
Alfa	Societa Anonima Lombarda Fabbrica Automobili (Lombardy Car Manufacturing Company, taken over by mining tycoon Nicola Romeo in 1915; hence Alfa Romeo)	Cars
BMW	Bayerische Motoren Werke (Bavarian Motor Works)	Cars and motorcycles
BSA	Birmingham Small Arms	Motorcycles
ERF	Edwin Richard Foden	Trucks
FAW	First Auto Works	Cars and trucks
Fiat	Fabbrica Italiana Automobili Torino (Italian Automobile Factory of Turin)	Cars, tractors, trucks and vans
FSO	Fabryka Samochodów Osobowyc (Passenger Car Factory)	Cars
GAZ	Gorkovsky Avtomobilny Zavod (Gorky Auto Plant)	Cars and trucks (including 4x4s)
GMC	General Motors Corporation	Trucks, SUVs and vans
IVECO	Industrial Vehicle Corporation	Trucks, buses and vans
LDV	Leyland Daf Vans	Vans and trucks
LTI	London Taxis International	Cabs
MAN	Maschinenfabrik Augsburg Nürnberg (Machinery Factories of Augsburg and Nuremberg)	Trucks
MBK	Motobécane (acronym created by new owner Yamaha)	Motorcycles, mopeds and scooters
MCI	Motor Coach Industries	Buses
MG	Morris Garages or Modern Gentleman	Cars
Saab	Svenska Aeroplan Aktiebolaget (Swedish Aircraft Ltd)	Cars
Seat	Sociedad Española de Automóviles de Turismo SA (Spanish Passenger Car Company)	Cars and vans
SYM	San Yang Motorcycles	Motorcycles
TVR	TreVoR (First name of Trevor Wilkinson, company founder)	Cars
VW	Volks Wagen [Volkswagen] (People's Car)	Cars and vans

Cars of the year

'Car of the Year' is a serious official accolade but, depending on where you are in the world, it can mean one of three entirely different models as chosen by leading (generally local) car writers. Honda has received the most honours of all (11), followed by Ford (10) and Fiat (7). Here are all the award-winners:

European Car of the Year

1964	Rover 2000
1965	Austin 1800
1966	Renault 16
1967	Fiat 124
1968	NSU Ro80
1969	Peugeot 504
1970	Fiat 128
1971	Citroën GS
1972	Fiat 127
1973	Audi 80
1974	Mercedes-Benz 450SE
1975	Citroën CX
1976	Simca 1307/Chrysler Alpine
1977	Rover 3500
1978	Porsche 928
1979	Simca/Chrysler Horizon
1980	Lancia Delta
1981	Ford Escort
1982	Renault 9
1983	Audi 100
1984	Fiat Uno
1985	Opel Kadett

1986	Ford Scorpio
1987	Opel Omega
1988	Peugeot 405
1989	Fiat Tipo *Illustrated below*
1990	Citroën XM
1991	Renault Clio
1992	Volkswagen Golf
1993	Nissan Micra
1994	Ford Mondeo
1995	Fiat Punto
1996	Fiat Bravo/Brava
1997	Renault Mégane Scénic
1998	Alfa Romeo 156
1999	Ford Focus
2000	Toyota Yaris
2001	Alfa Romeo 147
2002	Peugeot 307
2003	Renault Mégane
2004	Fiat Panda
2005	Toyota Prius
2006	Renault Clio
2007	Ford S-Max

North American Car of the Year

1994	Mercedes-Benz C-Class
1995	Chrysler Cirrus
1996	Chrysler/Dodge minivan
1997	Mercedes-Benz SLK
1998	Chevrolet Corvette
1999	Volkswagen Beetle
	Illustrated opposite
2000	Ford Focus
2001	Chrysler PT Cruiser
2002	Nissan Altima
2003	Mini Cooper
	Illustrated below
2004	Toyota Prius
2005	Chrysler 300
2006	Honda Civic
2007	Saturn Aura

North American Truck of the Year

1994	Dodge Ram
1995	Chevrolet Blazer
1996	Ford F-150
1997	Ford Expedition
1998	Mercedes-Benz ML320
1999	Jeep Grand Cherokee
2000	Nissan Xterra
2001	Acura MD-X
2002	Chevrolet Trailblazer
2003	Volvo XC90
2004	Ford F-150
2005	Ford Escape
2006	Honda Ridgeline
2007	Chevrolet Silverado

Japan Car of the Year

(only Japanese cars eligible)

1980–81	Mazda Familia
1981–82	Toyota Soarer
1982–83	Mazda Capella
1983–84	Honda Civic/Ballade
1984–85	Toyota MR2
1985–86	Honda Accord/Vigor
1986–87	Nissan Pulsar/Langley
1987–88	Mitsubishi Galant
1988–89	Nissan Silvia
1989–90	Toyota Celsior
1990–91	Mitsubishi Diamante
1991–92	Honda Civic
1992–93	Nissan Micra
1993–94	Honda Accord
1994–95	Mitsubishi FTO
1995–96	Honda Civic
1996–97	Mitsubishi Galant
1997–98	Toyota Prius
1998–99	Toyota Altezza
1999–2000	Toyota Vitz
2000–01	Honda Civic
2001–02	Honda Fit (Jazz)
2002–03	Honda Accord
2003–04	Subaru Legacy
2004–05	Honda Legend
2005–06	Mazda MX-5
2006–07	Lexus LS

The cars of the century

In August 1999 *Classic & Sports Car* magazine asked its readers to nominate their 'car of the century' – the twentieth century, that is. Here's how they voted:

1	Mini
2	Ford Model T
3	Volkswagen Beetle
4	Jaguar E-type
5	Ferrari 250 SWB
6	Porsche 911
7	Citroën DS
8	Mercedes-Benz 300SL
9	Rolls-Royce 40/50 hp Silver Ghost
10	Citroën 2CV
11	Lamborghini Miura
12	Jaguar Mk2
13	Willys Jeep
	Illustrated below
14	Lotus Elan
15	Audi Quattro
16	Aston Martin DB4
17	Jensen FF
18	Austin Seven
19	Jaguar XK120
20	NSU Ro80

The full grid of *The Wacky Races*

The classic children's cartoon show, made between 1968 and 1970 by American animation masters Hanna-Barbera and endlessly repeated ever since, was inspired by the movie *The Great Race*. Dick Dastardly never won a single race, but can you remember the full line-up on the starting grid of each of the 34 cartoons? Don't worry – here it is:

Entrant	Car
Ant Hill Mob	Bulletproof Bomb (aka The Roaring Plenty)
Dick Dastardly and Muttley	Mean Machine
Gruesome Twosome	Creepy Coupé
Luke and Blubber Bear	Arkansas Chugabug
Penelope Pitstop	Compact Pussycat
Peter Perfect	Turbo Terrific
Professor Pat Pending	Convert-A-Car
Red Max	Crimson Haybailer
Rufus Ruffcut and Sawtooth	Buzz Wagon
Sergeant Blast and Private Meekly	Army Surplus Special (aka The Surplus Six)
The Slag brothers (Rock & Gravel)	Boulder Mobile

The only production cars with V16 engines

The V16 engine, while certainly an engineering masterpiece, cannot significantly beat the smoothness of the less complex V12. This is why, despite the appearance of numerous prototypes and concept cars, there have only ever been three V16-engined production models.

Car	Year introduced	Country	Engine capacity	Number made
Cadillac V16	1930	USA	7420 cc	4387
Marmon V16	1931	USA	8046 cc	390
Cizeta V16T	1991	Italy	5995 cc	8

A celebration of slowness

No one ever bought a car expressly for its low top speed, even though one car (Britain's Trojan, launched in 1922) was actually sold under the slogan 'Can you afford to walk?', based on the comparative costs of running the car for 200 miles (322 km) versus the cost in shoe leather and socks. Still, the average male walking pace is 3½ mph (5.6 km/h), so how much faster is fast enough? Here are five extremely slow motor cars:

- The 1938 Rytecraft Scootacar was actually a roadgoing version of a fairground roundabout car. The London manufacturer fitted a 98-cc single-cylinder engine more usually found in chainsaws and lawnmowers, and it could just about make 15 mph (24 km/h).

- Britain enforced a national speed limit of 20 mph (32 km/h) between 1903 and 1930, and Rolls-Royce launched a car, the 1905 Legalimit, in which no owner could ever be caught speeding because it was governed to 20 mph. It was a total failure.

- There was a tiny, three-wheeled contraption called a Fend Flitzer built in Germany in 1948 that used human pedal-power to turn its bicycle wheels; many were driven by invalids. Other pedal-powered 'cars' were built and used in fuel-starved Paris during World War II.

- Only one production car since World War II has had a quoted top speed of 20 mph: the BMA Hazelcar, a tiny, electrically powered convertible built in Hove, East Sussex, between 1952 and 1957. Just six were sold, at £535 each.

- Even slower was another electric car, the Sinclair C5, launched unsuccessfully in 1985. With its three wheels, grey plastic body and handlebar steering, the C5 could make 15 mph (24 km/h), although the 15-mile range was somewhat optimistic.

The international guises of the Austin Seven

The 'Baby' Austin was first launched in 1922, and proved such an attractive proposition for budget motorists that manufacturers from outside Britain clamoured to take out licences to produce it. Japan's 1932 Datsun, often said to be a licence-built car, was in fact a close but unrelated copy of the Austin Seven. Here's a list of all the licensed versions:

Country	Car	Years in production
UK	Austin Seven *Illustrated below*	1922–39
FRANCE	Rosengart	1928–39
GERMANY	Dixi/BMW-Dixi	1928–32
USA	American Austin/Bantam	1930–41

The most expensive car book ever published

Only 10 copies of the 'special edition' of *Ferrari in Camera: From Ascari to Villeneuve* were published in 2001 by Palawan Press. With a painted metal cover, aluminium edging and a vellum spine, each book cost £2500. Other editions of this sumptuous photographic book were more attainable, however: one hundred 'leather' edition copies cost £1000 each, and the 890 'standard' editions were £350 each.

'Dormant' car brands owned by today's manufacturers

Hundreds of different companies have merged to form the dozen or so large car manufacturers that exist today around the world. That means that many old brand names lie disused in the bottom drawer of filing cabinets worldwide; here is a rummage through them:

Manufacturer	Brand name	Year last used
BMW	Glas	1968
	Riley	1969
	Triumph	1984
DaimlerChrysler	Hudson	1957
	Nash	1957
	De Soto	1960
	Imperial	1975
	Plymouth	2001
Fiat	OM	1939
	Autobianchi	1996
	Innocenti	1996
Ford	Lanchester	1956
	Rover	2005
General Motors	La Salle	1940
	Oldsmobile	2004
Nanjing	Wolseley	1976
	Austin	1987
	Morris	1984
Peugeot	Panhard	1967
	Singer	1969
	Hillman	1976
	Humber	1976
	Sunbeam	1976
	Talbot	1986
Renault/Nissan	Prince	1966
	Datsun	1985
	Alpine	1995
Toyota	Hino	1967
Volkswagen	Horch	1939
	Wanderer	1939
	DKW	1966
	Auto Union	1969
	NSU	1977

The V8 engine that goes on and on

General Motors' all-aluminium V8 engine, designed in the late 1950s, was introduced in these models:

Car	Type	Year	Power
Buick Skylark	sedan	1961	155 bhp
Oldsmobile Cutlass	sedan	1961	155 bhp
Pontiac Tempest	sedan	1961	155 bhp
Oldsmobile Jetfire Turbo	coupé/convertible	1962	215 bhp

The power unit had a short life in the United States, however, and was subsequently acquired by Rover in 1965. Since that time, this remarkable engine has powered all the vehicles below, in many states of tune, and is still manufactured in Britain today.

Car	Type	Year	Power
Rover P5B	saloon	1967	150 bhp
GKN-Lotus Type 47D	prototype	1968	296 bhp
Morgan Plus 8	roadster	1968	150 bhp
Rover P6B	saloon	1968	180 bhp
Rover P6BS	prototype	1968	180 bhp
Range Rover	SUV	1970	135 bhp
MGB GT V8	coupé	1973	137 bhp
Leyland P76 4.4	saloon	1974	192 bhp
Land Rover 101	military vehicle	1975	135 bhp
Rover SD1	saloon	1976	137 bhp
Land Rover 109	utility vehicle	1979	91 bhp
Triumph TR8	coupé	1979	132 bhp
Triumph TR8 injection	coupé	1979	137 bhp
Tara	prototype	1980	132 bhp
Rover SD1 Vitesse	saloon	1982	190 bhp
Land Rover 110	utility vehicle	1983	114 bhp
Morgan Plus 8 injection	roadster	1983	180 bhp
TVR 350i	coupé/roadster	1983	197 bhp
Escaro	all-terrain vehicle	1984	114 bhp
Marcos Spider 3.9	roadster	1984	190 bhp
TVR 390 SE	coupé/roadster	1984	275 bhp
Land Rover 90	utility vehicle	1985	114 bhp
Range Rover injection	SUV	1985	184 bhp
Sherpa 400 series	van/ambulance	1985	132 bhp
TVR 420 SEAC	roadster	1986	300 bhp
Land Rover 90/110	utility vehicle	1987	134 bhp

Sisu	all-terrain vehicle	1987	184 bhp
TVR 450 SE	roadster	1988	320 bhp
TVR Tuscan	race car	1988	400 bhp
Land Rover Discovery	SUV	1989	165 bhp
Range Rover 3.9	SUV	1989	184 bhp
Westfield SEiGHT	roadster	1989	207 bhp
Morgan Plus 8 3.9	roadster	1990	184 bhp
TVR S 4.0	roadster	1990	240 bhp
Cirrus	prototype	1991	198 bhp
Ginetta G33	roadster	1991	184 bhp
Mirach sports car	roadster	1991	250 bhp
Pegaso Z103	roadster	1991	184 bhp
PGO sports car	roadster	1991	184 bhp
TVR Griffith 4.0	roadster	1991	240 bhp
TVR Griffith 4.5	roadster	1991	286 bhp
MG RV8	roadster	1992	190 bhp
Range Rover LSE 4.2	SUV	1992	240 bhp
TVR Chimaera 4.0	roadster	1992	240 bhp
TVR Chimaera 5.0	roadster	1992	340 bhp
TVR Griffith 500 5.0	roadster	1992	340 bhp
Land Rover Defender	utility vehicle	1994	164 bhp
Marcos LM500	roadster	1994	320 bhp
Range Rover (new) 4.0	SUV	1994	190 bhp
Range Rover (new) 4.6	SUV	1994	225 bhp
LDV Convoy	van/ambulance	1996	144 bhp

The first 12 family hatchbacks and their numbers of doors

One or two early cars had had a rear door or tailgate, but the Renault 4 was the first to offer the feature in conjunction with the ability either to fold or to remove the rear seats to increase cargo capacity massively. The 'hatchback' was born and quickly imitated. Unfortunately, contemporary road-test reports, unlike those today, didn't measure the increase in boot space, but in most cases it was at least doubled.

1961	**Renault 4**	five doors
1962	**Innocenti A40S**	three doors
1964	**Autobianchi Primula**	three or five doors
1965	**Renault 16** *Illustrated below*	five doors
1967	**Simca 1100**	three or five doors
1967	**Citroën Dyane**	five doors
1968	**Renault 6**	five doors
1969	**Austin Maxi**	five doors
1970	**AMC Gremlin**	three doors
1971	**Fiat 127**	three doors
1972	**Renault 5**	three doors
1972	**Honda Civic**	three doors

The car as art

Cars have indeed been truly accepted as works of art. In 1951 the Museum of Modern Art (MoMA) in New York organized an exhibition entitled simply *Eight Automobiles*. Its curator, Arthur Drexler, selected the cars to illustrate his belief they were 'rolling sculpture'. They were:

• **Bentley 4½-litre**	1939		• **Mercedes-Benz SS**	1930
• **Cisitalia 202**	1947		• **MG TC**	1948
• **Cord 812**	1937		• **Talbot-Lago**	1939
• **Lincoln Continental**	1941		• **Willys Jeep**	1951

The Cisitalia (*illustrated below*, at MoMA) was the only one to remain in MoMA's permanent collection, but it was later joined by a Ferrari F1 car and, in 1996, a Jaguar E-type donated by Jaguar Cars, which the museum declared 'the most beautiful car in the world'. In 1963 MoMA also showcased an Italian sports car, the De Tomaso Vallelunga. Then in 1999 the museum staged *Different Roads: Automobiles for the Next Century*, featuring nine production and concept cars showcasing new structures and materials. These cars included:

• **Audi AL2 concept**	• **MCC Smart**
• **Chrysler CCV concept**	• **Rover Mini concept**
• **Ford Ka**	

In addition, in order to showcase new powerplants, the exhibition also featured:

• **Fiat Multipla**	• **Honda Insight**
• **GM EV1**	• **Toyota Prius**

In Paris, the Louvre displayed the Renault 16, one of the first five-door family hatchbacks, in 1965. Five years later, it exhibited a new Range Rover, eulogized as an example of 'modern sculpture'. In October 1982 an early exhibition at the Boilerhouse Project (the precursor to the Design Museum in London and initially based at the Victoria & Albert Museum) was devoted to the design of the Ford Sierra.

The most important car safety innovations

An on-the-spot poll of 1100 drivers conducted by Avon Tyres in 2006 revealed that more than one-quarter of them recognized the seatbelt as the most important car safety innovation of the twentieth century. These are the poll results:

1 Seatbelt	**27%**
2 Anti-lock braking system (ABS)	**21%**
3 Airbag	**16%**
4 Cat's eyes	**10%**
5 Crumple zones	**7%**
6 Three-point rear centre seatbelt	**6%**
7 Traction control	**3%**
=8 Side-impact protection bars	**2%**
=8 Emergency braking system (EBS)	**2%**
=8 Speed cameras	**2%**

Those polled were right to vote for the seatbelt. The three-point seatbelt, invented by Volvo's chief safety officer, Nils Bohlin, in 1958, is lauded by the National Highway Traffic Safety Administration in the United States. According to the agency, each year 11,000 lives are saved by the three-point seatbelt on American roads. Meanwhile, one of Volvo's own research projects has found that the invention has saved a million lives.

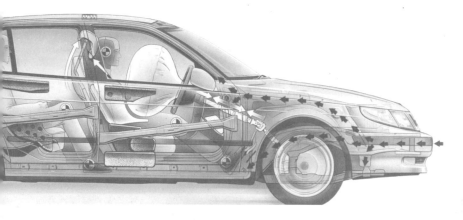

Owners' manuals: not exactly light reading ...

The Lexus GS 450h is the first petrol-electric luxury saloon, and every vehicle comes with an owner's manual explaining the car's functions in minute detail. At 494 pages, the manual is one of the longest ever published. There are 18 pages on 'Opening, closing and locking the doors and trunk'. Three pages are devoted to a signed declaration from Fujitsu that the anti-theft system meets telecoms directives – in 18 languages – while a daunting 15 pages cover checking and replacing fuses. Twenty-six pages into the Lexus GS 450h manual, you'll even find advice on how to scrap the car.

Fortunately, the section on the car's hybrid system begins on page eight, giving a resumé of how it works. But once you've understood that this car can be driven much like any other, you might start to skim other sections ... and become alarmed at the hundreds of panels headed '! CAUTION' and '! NOTICE'. Many of these relate to conceivable, albeit unlikely, outcomes of doing something mad, such as: 'Do not touch the high-voltage socket while the headlights are turned on. 20,000v is momentarily generated and may cause severe injury by electric shock.' Other directives seem unnecessarily obvious: 'Do not spill fuel during refuelling', or 'When taking a nap in the vehicle, always turn the hybrid system off.'

Carmakers who became
famous for other things

These companies found that carmaking took a back seat to other more profitable ventures, in which they eventually made their names:

Company	Year last car made	Better known for
Adler, Germany	1939	typewriters
Alvis, UK	1967	tanks
Hispano Suiza, Spain	1938	aircraft engine parts
Maytag, USA	1915	washing machines
Miele, Germany	1914	kitchen appliances

The 20 greatest car movies and their stars

These cinematic gems feature some truly memorable performances, not just from actors but also from cars.

Film	Car and stars
Genevieve, 1953	Darracq; Alan and Wendy McKim (John Gregson and Dinah Sheridan)
The Fast Lady, 1962	Bentley 3-litre; Charles Chingford (James Robertson Justice)
Carry on Cabby, 1963	Ford Cortina; Charlie and Peggy Hawkins (Sid James and Hattie Jacques)
Goldfinger, 1964	Aston Martin DB5; James Bond (Sean Connery)
The Yellow Rolls-Royce, 1964	Rolls-Royce Phantom 1; Marquess of Frinton (Rex Harrison)
The Graduate, 1967	Alfa Romeo Duetto Spider; Benjamin Braddock (Dustin Hoffman)
Bullitt, 1968	Ford Mustang GT390; Frank Bullitt (Steve McQueen)
The Love Bug, 1968	Volkswagen Beetle ('Herbie'); Jim Douglas (Dean Jones)
The Italian Job, 1969	BMC Mini Cooper; Charlie Croker (Michael Caine)
Duel, 1971	Plymouth Valiant; David Mann (Dennis Weaver)
The French Connection, 1971	Pontiac Le Mans; Jimmy 'Popeye' Doyle (Gene Hackman)
Le Mans, 1971	Porsche 917; Michael Delaney (Steve McQueen)

Vanishing Point, 1971	Dodge Challenger; Kowalski (Barry Newman)
The Spy Who Loved Me, 1977	Lotus Esprit; James Bond (Roger Moore)
Ferris Bueller's Day Off, 1986	Ferrari 250 California replica; Ferris Bueller (Matthew Broderick)
Tucker: The Man and His Dream, 1988	Tucker Torpedo; Preston Tucker (Jeff Bridges)
Driving Miss Daisy, 1989	Hudson Hornet; Daisy Werthen and Hoke Colburn (Jessica Tandy and Morgan Freeman)
Thelma & Louise, 1991	Ford Thunderbird; Thelma Dickinson and Louise Sawyer (Geena Davis and Susan Sarandon)
Gone in 60 Seconds, 2000	Shelby Mustang GT-500 (plus 49 other cars); Randall 'Memphis' Raines (Nicolas Cage)
The Fast and the Furious, 2001	Toyota Supra; Brian O'Connor (Paul Walker)
Who Killed the Electric Car?, 2006	GM EV1; Ed Begley Jr (Ed Begley Jr)

Are you sitting comfortably? Unlikely ...

There's no such thing as the perfect driving position, no matter how expensive or luxurious the car. The human body is not well suited to sitting behind a steering wheel. Once the body has been in any fixed posture for 15 minutes, the heart rate slows and muscles start to ache as lactic acid builds up in them and fails to be dissipated by movement. Poor driving posture is likely to cause the most damage to a driver's lower back. One study found that people spending four or more hours a day driving were six times more likely than pedestrians to need time off work on account of lower-back pain.

An ergonomically sound driving position offers – often with the help of seat adjustments – supportive cushioning on all the bony areas of the lumbar spine, hips and pelvis; good lateral thigh support also helps. Once sitting comfortably, you should be able to reach the pedals without stretching; the steering wheel should be centrally located in front of you to keep your spine straight, and the mirrors properly adjusted. Relaxed shoulders, and hands gripping the steering wheel just tightly enough, also improve posture. Ergonomists agree on the simplest avoidance tactic of all. Tina Worthy, a consultant ergonomist specializing in seating, says: 'More breaks, more frequently. Stopping, say, every hour to get more oxygen into your body by moving around really helps.'

Chinese copies

China's burgeoning motor industry has gained, in some quarters, notoriety for closely copying well-known Western models. 'Nobody's figured out quite how to deal with China yet', says Jay Nagley, of consultancy Spyder Automotive, an expert on the Chinese car industry. 'There is tension between those who want to "go legit" and those who want to continue ripping people off. These cars aren't a huge threat in Europe, but the United States could strike trade agreements with China that might include tightening the intellectual property rights situation in the country.' Here are the nine worst offenders:

Chinese car	Western model
Chery QQ	Chevrolet/Daewoo Matiz
Geely Merie	Mercedes-Benz C-Class
Geely Xaili/Haoqing	Daihatsu Charade (c. 1987)
Hongqi HQD	Rolls-Royce Phantom
Jiangling Landwind	Isuzu MU/Opel-Vauxhall Frontera
Shanghai Maple Hissoon 205	Citroën ZX
ShuangHuan Laibao	Honda CR-V Mk2
Zhejiang UFO	Toyota RAV4
Zotye 2008	Daihatsu Terios Mk1

The galling truth about map-reading

Matthew Joint, a behavioural psychologist at Britain's Automobile Association, compiled a major report from academic research in 1996 that concluded that men have superior 'visual-spatial' skills to women. This makes men better at navigating unfamiliar territory, while women are more likely to stop and ask for directions. Joint found that, during the foetal stage of development, testosterone levels affect the brain; women have less testosterone than men, tipping them more towards verbal skills. In 2005 scientists at the University of New Mexico pinpointed the difference on 'grey matter' (the information-processing brain tissue) or 'white matter' (tissue good for mental connectivity, language and multi-tasking). They found that men use 6.5 times as much grey matter as women; by comparison, women use far more of their white matter.

10 unusual awards for cars and car companies

Carmakers love to boast when they win awards. Here are some you might not have heard about ...

Aston Martin	Award for Excellence from the Luxury Briefing Awards, 2005, for the overall excellence of the marque's products and quality.
Austin Metro	Design Council Award, 1980, for its clever interior packaging.
Cadillac BLS	Best Winter Car from *Tekniikan Maailma* magazine, 2007, for its ability to stand up to harsh Arctic weather.
Honda Civic Hybrid	World Green Car from the World Car Awards, 2006, for its environmentally friendly drivetrain.
Plymouth Voyager	Excellence in Corrosion Protection Award from the Zinc Institute, 1984, for the MPV's sturdy rust-resistance.
Rover 75	World's Most Beautiful Automobile Award from Italian design writers' 'Design in Motion' panel, 2000, for its chic and stylish lines.
Saab 9-5 Biopower	Best of What's New Award from *Popular Science* magazine, 2005, for its bio-ethanol-fuelled engine.
Toyota	Customer Satisfaction Survey (first winner) from J.D. Power & Associates, 1981, for beating all rivals at keeping customers happy.
Toyota Prius	Global 500 commendation from the UN Environment Programme, 1999, for its pollution-cutting hybrid drive system.
Vauxhall Calibra Turbo	Tow Car of the Year Award from the Caravan Club (UK), 1993, for its trailer-pulling prowess (despite being a sporty coupé).

Car-type acronyms – hit or miss?

Only two of these technical-sounding acronyms, all created by carmakers, have made it into the everyday argot of motoring:

AAV	All-Activity Vehicle, Mercedes-Benz M-Class concept, 1996	**Miss**
CCV	China Concept Vehicle, Chrysler developing-markets concept, 1997	**Miss**
MPV	Multi-Purpose Vehicle, Mazda production car, 1988	**Hit**
MUV	Multi-Utility Vehicle, Tata Safari production car, 1998	**Miss**
OLV	Outdoor Lifestyle Vehicle, Hyundai concept, 2003	**Miss**
SAV	Sport Activity Vehicle, BMW X5 production car, 1999	**Miss**
SUT	Sport Utility Truck, Hummer production car, 2005	**Miss**
SUV	Sport Utility Vehicle, International Harvester Scout production car, 1961	**Hit**
TCV	Tourer Concept Vehicle, Rover concept, 2002	**Miss**
XUV	Crossover Utility Vehicle, GMC Envoy production car/pick-up, 2003	**Miss**

Same car, different title

They call it 'badge engineering' – building one car and then selling it under multiple, ostensibly different identities. These three machines have been sold under more different titles than any others in motoring history.

The original
Morris 1100/1300 (1962)

Also sold as
Austin 1100/1300
Innocenti J5
MG 1100/1300
Illustrated below
Riley Kestrel
Vanden Plas 1100/1300
Wolseley 1100/1300

The original
Hillman Avenger (1970)

Also sold as
Chrysler Avenger
Dodge 1500
Plymouth Cricket
Sunbeam 1250/1500
Talbot Avenger
Volkswagen 1500

The original
Chevrolet Cavalier (1981)

Also sold as
Buick Skyhawk
Cadillac Cimarron
Holden Camira
Isuzu Aska
Vauxhall Cavalier
Oldsmobile Firenza
Opel Ascona

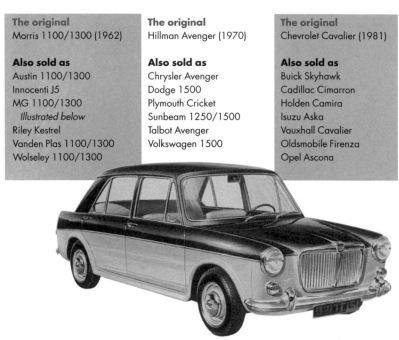

Turbocharger or supercharger?

A turbocharger is a mechanical device designed to boost engine power. It uses waste exhaust gases to drive a turbine, which in turn forces air into the combustion chambers. This then increases the throughput and hence the power available.

A supercharger is also a mechanical device that boosts engine power. In contrast to a turbocharger, however, it is an engine-driven compressor, achieving exactly the same end result.

Vehicle design courses

Want to create your own car, but don't know where to start? These institutions and courses can help you become one of the car designers of tomorrow:

Art Center College of Design, Pasadena, California, USA – transportation design

Cleveland Institute of Art, Ohio, USA – industrial/transportation design

College for Creative Studies, Detroit, Michigan, USA – transportation design

Coventry University School of Art and Design, West Midlands, UK – transportation design

Cranfield University, Bedfordshire, UK – automotive product engineering

École Espera Sbarro, Pontarlier, France – car design

Fachhochschule Pforzheim, Germany – transportation design

Institut Supérieur de Design, Valenciennes, France – transportation design

Marbella Design Academy, Spain – automotive design

Pratt Institute School of Art & Design, New York, USA – transportation design

Queens University, The Automotive Design Centre at Northern Ireland Technology Centre, Belfast, UK – industrial and materials training

Royal College of Art, London, UK – vehicle design

Scuola Politecnica di Design, Milan, Italy – transportation and car design

Umeå Institute of Design, Sweden – industrial/transportation design

University of Huddersfield School of Art & Design, Yorkshire, UK – transportation design

Weber State University, Center for Automotive Science and Technology, Ogden, Utah, USA – vehicle emissions and fuels

Green promises that have been broken

In both the United States and Britain, politicians promise much and deliver little. Here are two cases in which the environment continues to pay the price for a lack of conviction.

- California's geography makes it highly prone to air pollution, and the state's Air Resources Board resolved to do something about this in 1990. It ordered that, by 1998, 2 per cent of all new vehicles sold there had to be Zero Emissions Vehicles, rising to 10 per cent by 2003. That meant, basically, electric cars, but political and industry opposition was enormous. The legal targets were quietly dropped, and the biggest seven carmakers were told to show a 'good faith effort'. The result? There are a few hundred electric cars available for leasing, but the gas-guzzlers march on regardless.

- In Britain, one of the upsides of buying a hybrid car, such as a Toyota Prius or a Honda Civic, or of converting your car to run on liquid-petroleum gas, was that these more environmentally friendly fuel alternatives entitled you to a rebate from the government's Energy Saving Trust – worth, in some cases, £1500. That was, until March 2005, when this 'green' Powershift initiative was abandoned as a result of a clash with EC rules (according to the government). Sales of LPG cars collapsed, and hybrid buyers lost a much-hyped incentive to go green.

The naming of the Nissan Cedric

Nissan's Cedric is one of the oldest nameplates on Japanese roads, having been introduced in 1960 and offered in 10 different versions since then. The name itself pays homage to English novelist Frances Hodgson Burnett. The hero of her book *Little Lord Fauntleroy* (1886) is Cedric, a New York boy who discovers he is the missing heir to an ancient English earldom. Cedric's velvety suits and lace collars, vividly described by the author, became fashionable for well-heeled American boys, and the book also became extremely popular in Japan. Executives at Nissan assumed everyone in the West had read it, and so selected the noble Cedric name for its cars – unaware that, by 1960, Cedric sounded comically dated. By 1966 the name was no longer used for export models. The Cedric of today, a conventional two-litre sedan, is sold mostly to taxi operators.

BMW's Art Cars

For more than 30 years, the German marque BMW has been creating motoring masterpieces. It has commissioned 16 'Art Cars' – examples of its output decorated by leading artists. These cars now form an important and unique collection by some of the world's most admired painters. Here they are, in date order:

Artist	Year	Car canvas
Alexander Calder	1975	3.0 CSL
Frank Stella	1976	3.0 CSL
Roy Lichtenstein	1977	320i
Andy Warhol	1979	M1
Ernst Fuchs	1982	635 CSi
Robert Rauschenberg	1986	635 CSi
Ken Done	1989	M3
Michael Jagamara Nelson	1989	M3
Matazo Kayama	1990	535i
César Manrique	1990	730i
Esther Mahlangu	1991	525i
A.R. Penck	1991	Z1
Sandro Chia	1992	3 Series racer
David Hockney *Illustrated below*	1995	850 CSi
Jenny Holzer	1999	V12 LMR
Olafur Eliasson	2006	H2R

When it all goes pop ...

Motoring and celebrities may seem like a match made in heaven, but when it all goes wrong, the results can be embarrassing. Witness the fiasco of the pairing between Toyota and the all-girl group Atomic Kitten. The lyrical Liverpool ladies had already endorsed Seats and MGs – including having the ZS Atomix limited edition named in their honour – when, in 2003, their management hooked them up to Toyota's Land Cruiser to promote a 'greatest hits' album. No sooner was the ink dry on the contract than the group broke up, never to work again ... which is not something that Toyota wants you to think will happen to its cars.

The first 10 multi-lane highways

Freeways, motorways, autostradas – they all amount to pretty much the same thing: long-distance roads with several lanes that have greatly opened up countries to car travel. These were the first ones in major developed countries:

ITALY	1924	Milan–Varese Autostrada dei laghi
GERMANY	1935	Frankfurt-am-Main–Darmstadt Autobahn
USA	1940	Pennsylvania Turnpike
SWEDEN	1953	Malmö–Lund Motorvag
FRANCE	1954	Paris–Lille A1 Autoroute
MEXICO	1958	Mexico City–Querétaro Autopista
UK	1958	Preston Bypass M6 Motorway
AUSTRALIA	1959	Kwinana Freeway
JAPAN	1964	Kobe–Nagoya Highway
SPAIN	1971	Seville–Cadiz Autopista

Ratio of cars to road space

How crowded are our roads today? This table uses available data to define the road space available per registered car in each country.

Country	Miles of roads	Car parc*	Road space per car
NEW ZEALAND	57,290	2,287,200	0.250 miles
CHINA	1,183,030	15,000,000	0.078 miles
BRAZIL	1,230,312	18,627,600	0.066 miles
LUXEMBOURG	18,758	314,600	0.059 miles
AUSTRALIA	567,310	10,940,000	0.051 miles
CANADA	874,888	18,123,891	0.048 miles
SOUTH AFRICA	223,044	4,574,972	0.048 miles
ICELAND	8098	175,427	0.046 miles
TURKEY	382,397	11,077,522	0.034 miles
IRELAND	57,476	1,660,000	0.034 miles
SWEDEN	130,959	4,156.647	0.031 miles
AUSTRIA	124,274	4,156,743	0.029 miles
NORWAY	56,383	2,028,909	0.027 miles
ARGENTINA	133,864	5,570,000	0.024 miles
RUSSIA	589,058	25,285,000	0.023 miles
DENMARK	44,388	1,870,500	0.023 miles
FINLAND	48,466	2,414,477	0.020 miles
BELGIUM	92,595	4,873,333	0.019 miles
FRANCE	555,069	30,100,000	0.018 miles
USA	2,299,069	133,880,000	0.017 miles
GREECE	72,700	4,204,500	0.017 miles
MEXICO	201,309	14,136,400	0.014 miles
JAPAN	715,946	57,090,789	0.012 miles
ITALY	406,796	34,667,485	0.011 miles
SWITZERLAND	44,153	3,863,807	0.011 miles
SPAIN	215,525	20,250,377	0.010 miles
THE NETHERLANDS	78,028	7,256,000	0.010 miles
PORTUGAL	42,708	4,200,000	0.010 miles
ISRAEL	17,237	1,800,000	0.009 miles
GERMANY	351,161	46,090,303	0.007 miles
UK	245,068	30,651,700	0.007 miles
SOUTH KOREA	86,990	11,122,200	0.007 miles
MONACO	31	23,720	0.001 miles

* 'Car parc' refers to the total number of cars in a given area.

Gullwing doors

Mercedes-Benz pioneered 'gullwing' doors on its 1954 300SL. The doors were so named on account of the shape of a seagull in mid-flight that was created when both doors were open. This was in fact a technical, rather than a styling, feature: the race-derived, space-frame chassis of the car made for a high sill at the sides, which would have been too high for conventional, front-hinged doors. Including the 300SL, there have been six gullwing production cars (not including kit cars):

1954	**Mercedes-Benz 300SL**	GERMANY
1960	**Marcos GT**	UK
1975	**Bricklin SV-1**	CANADA
1981	**Delorean DMC-12**	NORTHERN IRELAND
1993	**Mazda Autozam AZ-1***	JAPAN
2003	**Bristol Fighter**	UK

* also sold as the Suzuki Cara

As an eye-catching feature on concept cars and prototypes, however, gullwing doors have been far more popular. In chronological order of unveiling, these have included:

1962	**Ford Cougar 406**	USA
1967	**Bertone/Lamborghini Marzal**	ITALY
1969	**Mercedes-Benz C111** *Illustrated opposite*	GERMANY
1971	**Italdesign/VW-Porsche 914 Tapiro**	ITALY
1972	**BMW Turbo**	GERMANY
1973	**Chevrolet Corvette 4-Rotor**	USA
1973	**Innes Lee Scorpion K-19**	UK
1974	**Michelotti Mizar/Lancia Beta**	ITALY
1975	**Gmarmeier/NSU Ro80**	GERMANY
1976	**Ghia/Ford Corrida**	ITALY
1980	**Aston Martin Bulldog**	UK
1980	**Citroën Karin**	FRANCE
1981	**Pohlmann EL**	GERMANY
1986	**Pontiac Trans Sport**	USA
1986	**Volkswagen Scooter**	GERMANY
1989	**Mazda TDR**	JAPAN

1991	**Mazda HR X2**	JAPAN
1991	**Mercedes-Benz C112**	GERMANY
1993	**Isdera Commendatore**	GERMANY
1993	**Karmann/Mercedes-Benz 300SL**	GERMANY
1994	**Bertone/Porsche Karisma**	ITALY
1996	**Pininfarina CNR Etabeta**	ITALY
1999	**BMW Z9**	GERMANY
2001	**Cree SAM**	SWITZERLAND
2001	**Renault Talisman**	FRANCE
2003	**Bertone Birusa**	ITALY
2003	**Daihatsu UFE-II**	JAPAN
2003	**Infiniti Triant**	USA/CANADA
2004	**Volvo YCC**	SWEDEN
2005	**Nissan Zaroot**	JAPAN
2005	**Toyota Fine-X and Fine-T**	JAPAN
2006	**Renault Nepta**	FRANCE
2007	**Ford Airstream**	USA
2007	**Mazda Ryuga**	JAPAN
2007	**Nissan Nagare**	JAPAN

The pitfall of the gullwing door in the 'real world' is revealed in bad weather: when opened during or after rain, the door may drip water and dirt on exiting occupants. This perhaps influenced the design of the 1990 Toyota Sera, a production car that featured semi-gullwing doors that tilted open diagonally via fixtures above the centre of the windscreen and on the door pillars. This feature has also been seen on several concept cars and prototypes. The 1996 Italdesign/Daewoo Bucrane concept boasted unique gullwing opening roof panels.

The high-octane world of *The Persuaders!*

The Persuaders!, a TV show first broadcast in Britain in autumn 1971, and a year later in the United States, delighted car enthusiasts. It followed the adventures of two playboys, American tycoon Danny Wilde (Tony Curtis) and British aristocrat Lord Brett Sinclair (Roger Moore), who drove, respectively, a Ferrari Dino 246 GT and an Aston Martin DBS. You may have watched it when you were a child, or seen it on DVD, but do you know these 10 nuggets?

(1) Filming of the 24 episodes of *The Persuaders!* began in June 1970.

(2) Aston Martin provided a six-cylinder DBS in Bahama yellow with a manual gearbox, but it was, visually, to the same specification as the then-new DBS V8, with alloy wheels instead of wires.

(3) Ferrari loaned a red Dino 246 GT with the Modena registration number of 221400-MO. Production supervisor Johnny Goodman personally collected the car from Maranello and drove it straight to the location set on the Côte d'Azur.

(4) While the Aston Martin and the Ferrari appeared prominently, Curtis and Moore drove many other vehicles, including Land Rovers, a Range Rover, BMW 3.0S, Mini Moke, Citroën H-type and Ford Econoline vans, and an AEC petrol tanker.

(5) There is a classic continuity blooper in *The Persuaders!* episode 'The Gold Napoleon' when Sinclair's Aston passes behind another vehicle wearing its false 'BS 1' number plates, only to emerge sporting the car's real registration of PPH 6H.

(6) Several driving sequences were actually shot in the Welsh mountains, doubling up for the hills in the south of France.

(7) *The Persuaders!* was the most expensive British TV series at the time, each episode costing £80,000. But critics were unimpressed. T.C. Worsley, writing in the *Financial Times* in 1971, said, 'If I had paid that sum and my writers came up with anything so childishly unconvincing as these stories, I should want to know why.'

(8) The show flopped in the United States, where ABC scheduled it against NBC's *Mission: Impossible,* but was a hit elsewhere.

⑨ The status of the Ferrari Dino used is obscure. It seems that the car Ferrari supplied was actually privately owned. Chassis number 00810, it was the 405th Dino built, completed in May 1970. The first registered owner was Giovanni Cavedoni of Modena, according to Swiss Ferrari historian Marcel Massini, and the Dino still exists in Italy today.

⑩ With filming over, the Aston was sold through London dealer H.R. Owen and had five owners before *The Persuaders!* aficionado Mike Sanders bought it in 1994. Aston Martin renovated it so perfectly that it is now recognized as one of the world's finest six-cylinder DBSs.

Crossply tyres

Crossply tyres, with criss-crossed layers of nylon instead of the superior steel belts of radials, are no longer fitted to any new car but are still manufactured for mostly pre-1960 classic and vintage models, to keep them authentic. They are not illegal, although it's not advisable to drive a car with any combination of radial and crossply tyres. According to the Tyre Industry Council, however, some aircraft, trucks in Africa and rugged former Eastern Bloc territories, and earth-moving and agricultural vehicles still use crossplies. Made by such firms as Michelin, Dunlop and Firestone, these tyres are better at resisting sidewall damage .

The 50 most powerful people in the car industry

In 2006 influential magazine *Car* compiled a list it called 'The Power 50' – 'the men and women whose decisions shape the world of cars'. As well as ranking individuals, it categorized them in five ways: 'beancounter' (*i.e.* accountant), 'car guy' (*i.e.* enthusiast), 'motoring royalty' (*i.e.* founder or major shareholder), 'racer' and 'designer'. Here they are:

1 **Carlos Ghosn** Chief Executive Officer of Nissan and Renault – beancounter

2 **Katsuaki Watanabe** President and Chief Executive Officer of Toyota – beancounter

3 **Bill Ford** Chairman and Chief Executive Officer of Ford – beancounter/motoring royalty

4 **Rick Wagoner** Chairman and Chief Executive Officer of General Motors – beancounter

5 **Dieter Zetsche** Chief Executive Officer of DaimlerChrysler – beancounter

6 **Chung Mong-Koo** Chairman of Hyundai – beancounter/motoring royalty

7 **Jean Martin-Folz** Chief Executive Officer of PSA Peugeot Citroën – beancounter

8 **Bernd Pischetsreider** Chief Executive Officer of Volkswagen – beancounter

9 **Takeo Fukui** Chief Executive Officer of Honda – beancounter/car guy/racer

10 **Sergio Marchionne** Chief Executive Officer of Fiat – beancounter

11 **Helmut Panke** Chairman of BMW – beancounter/car guy

12 **Mark Fields** President of Ford of the Americas – beancounter

13 **Tom LaSorda** Chief Executive Officer of Chrysler Group – beancounter

14 **Bob Lutz** Vice-chairman of Global Product Development of General Motors – beancounter/car guy

15 **Jim Padilla** President and Chief Operating Officer of Ford – beancounter

16 **Wolfgang Bernhard** Chief Executive Officer of Volkswagen – beancounter

17 **Chen Xianglin** Chief Executive Officer of Shanghai Automotive Industries Corporation – beancounter

18 **Lewis Booth** Executive Vice-president of Ford of Europe and Ford's Premier Automotive Group (which includes Volvo, Jaguar, Land Rover, and [at the time] Aston Martin) – beancounter

19 **Carl Peter Forster** Chairman of General Motors Europe – beancounter

20 **Osamu Suzuki** Chairman and Chief Executive Officer of Suzuki – beancounter/motoring royalty

21 **Martin Winterkorn** Chairman of Audi – beancounter

22 **Ferdinand Piech** Chairman of Volkswagen – beancounter/car guy/motoring royalty

23 **Wendelin Wiedeking** Chief Executive Officer of Porsche – beancounter

24 **Richard Parry-Jones** Vice-president of Global Product Development of Ford – car guy/racer

25 **Osamu Masuko** President of Mitsubishi Motors – beancounter

26 **Hisakazu Imaki** President and Chief Executive Officer of Mazda – beancounter

27 **Burkhard Goeschel** BMW board member in charge of development – car guy

28 **Steve Miller** Chairman and Chief Executive Officer of parts maker Delphi – beancounter

29 **Ron Gettelfinger** President of America's Union of Auto Workers – car guy

30 **Nick Reilly** President and Chief Executive Officer of GM Daewoo – beancounter

31 **Zhu Yangleng** President of First Auto Works, Chinese carmaker – beancounter

32 **Kirk Kerkorian** Las Vegas billionaire and car industry investor – beancounter

33 **Kevin Wale** President and Managing Director of General Motors China – beancounter

34 **Fritz Henderson** Vice-chairman and Chief Financial Officer of General Motors – beancounter

35 **Scott Sprinzen and Bruce Clark** Analysts at Standard & Poor's and Moody's respectively – beancounters

36 **Luca di Montezemolo** President of Fiat and Ferrari – beancounter/racer

37 **J. Mays** Vice-president of Design and Chief Creative Officer at Ford – designer

38 **Toshiako Kamimura** President of Japan Trust Service Bank, which holds a stake in Toyota, Nissan, Mazda and Isuzu – beancounter

39 **Max Mosley** President of the Fédération Internationale de l'Automobile, motor-sport governing body and car-safety assessment organization – beancounter/racer

40 **Bernie Ecclestone** Chief Executive Officer of Formula One Group, in control of Formula One – beancounter/racer

41 **Roger Penske** Chairman of Penske Corporation, Indy 500 team – beancounter/racer

42 **Anne Stevens** Chief Operating Officer of Ford of the Americas – beancounter

43 **John and Lapo Elkann** Deputy Chairman of Fiat and Director of Brand Promotions at Fiat respectively – motoring royalty

44 **Michael Smith** Chairman of CVC Capital Partners, which controls Formula One – beancounter

45 **Johanna Quandt** Heiress who ultimately runs BMW – beancounter/motoring royalty

46 **Ratan N. Tata** Chairman of Tata Sons (Indian carmaking conglomerate) – beancounter/motoring royalty

47 **Michael Schumacher** Seven times Formula One World Champion – racer

48 **Ed Wellburn** Vice-president of Design at General Motors – designer

49 **Fernando Alonso** Formula One World Champion – racer

50 **David Richards** Non-executive Director, World Rally Championship, Chairman, International Sportsworld Communicators (ISC) and Chairman of Prodrive – beancounter/racer

Let there be light

Audi's new 187-mph (300-km/h) R8 supercar, a mid-engined two-seater intended to rival the Porsche 911, has plenty of head-turning facets. One of the most spectacular is its lighting. It has a total of 24 light-emitting diode (LED) daytime driving lamps at the front. The headlamp units, with 12 LEDs ranged on either side, are inspired by the pronounced curves of the Sydney Opera House. Meanwhile, 186 LED tail lights at the back give exceptional visibility to other drivers, especially when the brakes are applied and they brighten.

An optional extra package of LEDs is available, not only to light the cabin, but also to bathe the V8 engine compartment – clearly visible to onlookers through its glass cover – in LED light.

Four more well-lit interiors

Coloured instrument lighting made its first appearance on the Jaguar MkVII sports saloon in 1950. The car's dashboard was backlit in purple, giving the cabin a violet glow at night.

The 1966 Jensen Interceptor was the first car to feature a timed delay for its interior lights, so that the light stayed on for a short time after the driver had sat down and shut the door.

The 1993 Lagonda Vignale show car, built by Ghia, featured 12-volt halogen spotlamps, some of the brightest map-reading lights ever fitted to a car, in addition to individual lights for its inbuilt rear writing tables.

Finished in brushed steel, the 2001 Lexus SC430 convertible has the distinction of being the first car in the world with an illuminated scuff plate in the door sill. A 'Lexus' script is lit up in it at night when the door is open.

The world's most venerable sports-car lines

There are sports cars and there are sports cars, but these iconic lines lead the world for longevity and reputation:

- **Alfa Romeo Spider**   **ITALY**

  First introduced as the Giulietta Spider in 1955; major model updates in 1966 (Duetto), 1994 and 2005.

- **Aston Martin DB**   **UK**

  First introduced as the DB1 in 1948; major model updates in 1950 (DB2), 1958 (DB4), 1967 (DBS), 1993 (DB7) and 2004 (DB9). *Illustrated below.*

- **Chevrolet Corvette**   **USA**

  First introduced as the Chevrolet Corvette in 1953; major model updates in 1963 (Sting Ray), 1968 (Sting Ray), 1983 and 1997.

- **Nissan Z**   **JAPAN**

  First introduced as the 240Z in 1969; major model updates in 1978 (280ZX), 1984 (300ZX), 1990 (300ZX) and 2002 (350Z).

- **Porsche 911**   **GERMANY**

  First introduced as the 911 in 1963; major model updates in 1989, 1997 and 2004.

The best way to stay awake behind the wheel

We are constantly told not to drive when we feel tired. But which is the best 'perk-up' – a hot beverage or an 'energy' drink? These are the relative caffeine contents of common 'stimulant' drinks:

Coffee	a 200-ml cup has 80 milligrams of caffeine
Red Bull	a 250-ml can has 80 milligrams of caffeine
Cola drinks	a typical can has 7–43 milligrams of caffeine
Tea	a 200-ml cup has 40 milligrams of caffeine
Hot chocolate	a 200-ml cup has 1–8 milligrams of caffeine

By comparison, a 50-gram chocolate bar has 6–21 milligrams of caffeine, but is also rich in the stimulant theobromine.

Leading nutrition expert Dell Stanford's optimum suggestion for any tired driver with normal health is to drink a caffé latte with skimmed milk, which provides caffeine and, from its milk, energy and calcium without the added-sugar downside of fizzy drinks. (An average daily caffeine intake of 300 milligrams is usually considered harmless.) A few squares of chocolate with a high cocoa content also raise your serotonin ('feel-good' chemical) levels. However, you should never drive if you feel too tired to do so.

25 top TV detectives and what they drive

Television detectives, whether official police or private investigators, have provided thrilling entertainment for more than five decades, and so have their cars. Here are the most memorable:

Show	Date aired	Detective	Car
Bergerac	1981–92	James Bergerac	Triumph 1800 Roadster
Charlie's Angels	1976–81	Sabrina Duncan (private)	Ford Pinto
		Jill Munroe (private)	Ford Mustang Cobra
Columbo	1971–78	Lt Columbo	Peugeot 403 cabriolet
Dempsey &	1985–86	Harriet Makepeace	Ford Escort cabriolet
Makepeace		James Dempsey	Mercedes-Benz 500SL
The Equalizer	1985–89	Robert McCall (private)	Jaguar XJ6
Hart to Hart	1979–84	Jonathan Hart (private)	Rolls-Royce Corniche
		Jennifer Hart (private)	Mercedes-Benz SL
The Inspector Lynley Mysteries	2001–07	Thomas Lynley	Bristol 410
Inspector Morse	1987–2000	Endeavour Morse	Jaguar MkII
Kojak	1973–78	Theo Kojak	Buick Regal
Life on Mars	2006–07	Gene Hunt	Ford Cortina Mk3
Magnum P. I.	1980–88	Thomas Magnum III (private)	Ferrari 308 GTS
Maigret	1960–63	Jules Maigret	Citroën 15-Six
Man in a Suitcase	1967	McGill (private)	Hillman Imp
Mannix	1967–75	Joe Mannix (private)	Oldsmobile Toronado
Miami Vice	1985–89	James Crockett	Ferrari Testarossa
Midsomer Murders	1997–2007	Tom Barnaby	Jaguar X-type
The Professionals	1977–81	Ray Doyle	Ford Escort RS 2000
		William Bodie	Ford Capri 3.0S
The Protectors	1972–74	Harry Rule (private)	Jensen Interceptor
		Contessa Caroline di Contini (private)	Citroën SM
Randall & Hopkirk (Deceased)	1969–70	Jeff Randall (private)	Vauxhall Victor FD
The Rockford Files	1974–80	Jim Rockford (private)	Pontiac Firebird
Saber of London	1955–61	Mark Saber (private)	Porsche 356
Shoestring	1979	Eddie Shoestring (private)	Ford Cortina Mk2
Starsky & Hutch	1975–79	Dave Starsky	Ford Gran Torino
		Ken Hutchinson	Ford Galaxie
The Sweeney	1975–78	Jack Regan	Ford Consul/Granada Mk2
		George Carter	Ford Cortina Mk3
Vega$	1978–81	Dan Tanna (private)	Ford Thunderbird Mk1

Foreign car plants in the United States

American industrialists embraced the automobile with open arms at the dawn of the twentieth century. Dozens of different marques competed for sales, and there was, with one very early exception, no room for outposts from other countries. In fact, only Rolls-Royce established a successful plant in the United States before World War II, and even that was short-lived. By the end of the 1970s, however, non-American companies had begun to establish North American plants, mostly to produce small, economical models. Here is a list of all the foreign 'transplants' ever established Stateside:

Manufacturer	Location	Year opened
Daimler	Queens, New York	1892 (closed 1907)
Rolls-Royce	Springfield, Massachusetts	1919 (closed 1931)
Volkswagen	Westmoreland County, Pennsylvania	1978 (closed 1988)
Honda	Marysville, Ohio	1982
Nissan	Smyrna, Tennessee	1983
Toyota (NUMMI)	Fremont, California	1984
Mazda	Flat Rock, Michigan	1987
Mitsubishi	Normal, Illinois	1988
Subaru/Isuzu	Lafayette, Indiana	1988 (Isuzu no longer involved)
Toyota	Georgetown, Kentucky	1988
Honda	Liberty, Ohio	1989
BMW	Spartanburg, South Carolina	1994
Mercedes-Benz	Tuscaloosa, Alabama	1997
Honda	Lincoln, Alabama	2001
Hyundai	Montgomery, Alabama	2005
Kia	West Point, Georgia	2009 (scheduled)

So what exactly is a spoiler?

Cars need to be streamlined if they're going to cleave their way through airflow efficiently. Streamlining makes a car go faster and can also improve fuel consumption dramatically.

Although it's pretty obvious that a 'slippery' teardrop-shaped car body has less wind resistance than a cubic one, another aspect has an important bearing on how a car performs on the road: stability. If a car has a streamlined shape but becomes unstable when it's driven fast, then its roadholding will be unpredictable – and that can make it unsafe.

A car's weight presses its tyres to the road, and one way to boost this grip – and with it, roadholding – is to increase the weight. But that makes cornering harder, because of the extra inertia, and that's where the science of aerodynamics comes in. By 'spoiling' airflow to the car's advantage, and pressing it down on to the tarmac, a spoiler increases its grip on the road.

A spoiler acts like an aircraft wing, but upside down, generating downforce instead of uplift. Air is forced both above and below a car as it drives along. A front spoiler, or air dam, usually fitted below the front bumper, prevents rushing air from getting under the car and unsettling it as speed increases.

Air, pushed over the bonnet and roof of a car as it travels, can loosen its roadholding, seriously affecting its road behaviour. Therefore, a rear spoiler is often fitted, ranging from a simple raised lip on the edge of the boot lid to elaborately designed wings supported by struts on either side of the boot. These aerofoils exert pressure on the back of the car, literally pushing it down on to the road surface.

Spoilers were fitted first to sports-racing and Formula One cars in the 1960s to boost their competitiveness; they then migrated to fast road cars, such as the 1974 Porsche 911 Turbo. Sometimes carmakers get their calculations wrong: the Audi TT was found to be unstable without a rear spoiler, and the design was altered to incorporate one after some fast-driving customers experienced alarming handling.

Architects who designed cars

The basic metal structure of a car is often called its 'architecture', but a few architects have had a go at designing a car of their own. Some of these vehicles have been sold to the public, but most have remained as one-offs.

Mario Bellini	Kar-A-Sutra minibus – 1972 *Illustrated below*
	Lancia Trevi (interior) – 1980
Pierre-Jules Boulanger	Citroën 2CV –1939
Ronald Aver Duncan	Stoneleigh –1928
Norman Foster	Solar electric minibus –1992
Richard Buckminster Fuller	Dymaxion – 1933
Naum Gabo	Jowett Javelin proposal – 1943
Walter Gropius	Adler Favorit cabriolet – 1930
	Adler Standard – 1931
Le Corbusier	'Voiture Minimum' – 1928
Carlo Mollino	Nardi Bisiluro – 1955
Robert Opron	Citroën SM – 1972
	Renault Fuego – 1980
Renzo Piano	Fiat VSS prototype – 1978

London's long battle with parking ...

Land in London is at a premium, so it is perhaps appropriate that the city has often led the way in the world of parking. For instance:

- The world's first multi-storey car park opened on Denman Street, off Piccadilly, in 1901. With an electric lift, seven floors and 19,000 square feet (1765 sq. m) of space, it was then also the world's biggest car park.

- In 1958 Britain's first parking meters were installed in Grosvenor Square, Mayfair. Three years later they were modified with spring-loaded mountings so that they could withstand abuse from outraged drivers.

- On the other side of town, meanwhile, 1961 also saw the opening of the 'Autostacker' in Woolwich, south-east London. This was a completely automated multi-storey car park, which could park 256 cars by conveyor belts, lifts and remote control. It cost £100,000 to build but closed just a year later, after all efforts had failed to make it work properly. Greenwich Council then spent £60,000 demolishing it.

... although Hastings was well ahead in the 1930s

- The world's first municipal car park opened in the United States in Flint, Michigan, in 1924, but it was Hastings Council in Sussex that – literally – broke new ground seven years later by opening the world's first underground car park. It's at Carlisle Parade and is still operating today.

The A–Z of car design

If you find yourself sitting next to a car designer on a long-haul flight, he (or she) might start telling you about his (or her) job. This guide to car-design jargon will help you understand what on earth he (or she) is talking about.

A is for A-pillar	A vertical roof-support post, sitting between the windscreen and front door. The B-pillar divides the front and rear doors; the C-pillar sits between the rear doors and rear window, hatchback or estate rear side windows; and the D-pillar (on an estate) sits between the rear side windows and tailgate.
B is for Box	One of the major volumetric components of car architecture. In a traditional saloon there are three boxes: one for the engine, one for the passengers, and one for the luggage.
C is for Cab Forward	The position of the passenger cell in a car's form, which determines its stance. A cab-forward design tends to suggest dynamism, while cab backwards denotes a more relaxed posture.
D is for DLO	Short for 'daylight opening', used by designers at an early stage to determine where a car's windows are positioned.
E is for Epowood	A hard, synthetic material used by designers to build realistic, full-size mock-up models.
F is for Frontal Area	The front end of the car determines how it slips through the air, affecting performance, economy and stability; the less frontal area there is – which is a design challenge – the better all three will be.
G is for Greenhouse	The glazed, upper part of the passenger cabin comprising the side windows and front and rear screens.
H is for Hardpoints	The frozen dimensions, surfaces, lines or points that define the car. These might include greenhouse pillar sections, the location of the spare wheel, or the side glass surface at the driver's eye level.
I is for Interiors	Car design is split between interiors and exteriors and, although interior design is of utmost importance to the car's functionality, working in exterior design is seen as more prestigious.
J is for Jaray	Unknown genius and Zeppelin designer Paul Jaray was the first to realize that aerodynamics actually made cars cut through the air more easily and therefore faster, and advocated that everything on cars should be 'faired-in'.
K is for Kamm	Aerodynamics pioneer Wunibald Kamm believed that a sharply truncated tail exploited the benefits of the low-pressure area behind a moving vehicle for better performance. Today a Kamm tail is any that is sharply cut-off.

L is for Lyons	William Lyons began by making motorcycle sidecars and ended up creating Jaguar. Although not a designer, he instinctively knew to the millimetre what made a saloon or sports car look perfect.
M is for Milling	A machine tool process. A numerically controlled milling machine interprets mathematical data from a digitizer and sculpts a three-dimensional model from wood or clay. This gives designers an accurate idea of how the real car will look.
N is for Notchback	A car with a clearly defined, saloon-type rear deck – as opposed to a hatchback.
O is for Overhang	The parts of a car anterior and posterior to the wheel arches.
P is for Package	The most demanding part in the design of any car is to achieve the maximum interior space within the smallest exterior. That is the package.
Q is for Le Quément	Renault design chief Patrick le Quément is, arguably, the man who brought design awareness to mass-market family cars during the 1990s with the Twingo, Clio and Mégane.
R is for Razor Edge	The origami school of car design, where sharp, geometrical forms and angles dominate the overall shape.
S is for Swage Line	An emphatic crease in a metal panel. Without swage lines, cars would look slab-sided and barrel-like.
T is for Tumblehome	The angle between the vertical and the greenhouse when seen from the front.
U is for Underbody	The bit car designers don't want you to see. This is the outer profile of the floorpan and is usually an unsightly mass of steel bumps and alcoves that accommodate such external fittings as the exhaust system.
V is for Valance	An apron at the front or back of a car often concealing the join between chassis and body, as well as carrying such items as lights and number-plate recesses.
W is for Wheel Arch	The bodywork aperture containing the wheels.
X is for Generation X	Or Ingredient X, the X Factor, Project X; this is the letter that finds its way on to almost all concept cars to denote them as special and different.
Y is for Youthful	All carmakers seek to make their designs 'youthful' in order to appeal to new customers and flatter older ones. The irony is that young buyers often have the least to spend on a car.
Z is for Zong	A word invented by the 'father' of car design, Harley Earl of General Motors, to describe certain body parts or specific aesthetic gestures. Along with other words, such as 'duflunky' and 'rashoom', it inspired 1930s design-studio staff.

The cars most name-dropped in rap songs

Agenda Inc., a popular-culture research company based in San Francisco, tracked every mention of brands in the lyrics of every single in *Billboard* magazine's Top 20 chart listing throughout 2005; there were 106 in all. There were more mentions of car brands than any other category, followed by fashion, weapons and alcoholic drinks. Thirty-five per cent of the songs that charted contained product references, with the top-of-the league Mercedes-Benz receiving 100 mentions, 37 more than Nike. Rapper 50 Cent was the biggest plugger (with 17 brands), mentioning, among others, Mercedes-Benz, Bentley and Lamborghini. Here's the ranking:

1	Mercedes-Benz	6	Hennessy
2	Nike	7	Chevrolet
3	Cadillac	=8	Louis Vuitton
4	Bentley	=8	Cristal
5	Rolls-Royce	10	AK-47

The 10 safest new cars – and why

According to calculations by *Forbes* magazine and the American not-for-profit safety-advice organization Informed for Life, these are the 2006 models in which occupants are least likely to suffer injury or death, as well as being the cars best equipped to avoid an accident in the first place. To achieve this, they need electronic stability control, which minimizes the risk of rollover, and side-impact (or side-curtain) airbags as the bare minimum. The best-performing vehicles also tend to be large, heavy saloons weighing more than 4000 pounds (1815 kg), which – unlike SUVs – have a low centre of gravity.

1	Acura RL	6	Lincoln Town Car
2	Volvo S80	7	Buick Lucerne
3	Honda Odyssey	8	Lexus ES330
4	Acura TL	9	Lincoln LS
5	Chrysler 300C/Dodge Charger	10	Honda Pilot

Porsche's classic designs ... that aren't cars

Porsche is world-renowned for its sports cars, but in 1972 it also helped establish the Porsche Design Group, in Austria, to design and market other products based on the company's ethos of excellence in precision engineering. By general consensus – and its own admission – Porsche Design has come up with many design classics, chief among which are the following:

CHRONOGRAPH 1 WATCH 1972

HELMET 1976

911 SUNGLASSES 1978

COMPASS WATCH 1978

SKI GOGGLES 1978 *Illustrated below*

CONCEPT BIKE 1979

TITANIUM CHRONOGRAPH 1979

OCEAN 2000 WATCH 1981

ANTROPOVARIUS LOUNGE CHAIR 1982

KANDIDO DESK LAMP 1982

IP84S LOUNGE CHAIR 1984

2001 TELEPHONE 1989

KETTLE 1997

TOASTER 1997

FINE PIX 6800 CAMERA 2001

READING GLASSES 2002

GRAND PIANO 2003

A short history of the car radio

These are the 10 key moments in the development of in-car radio:

1 **First factory-fitted radio – 1922**
First appeared in the UK (made by Marconi) and USA (Van Nuys 'Motoradio').

2 **First radio as standard equipment – 1934**
This was a Philco unit, made by Dutch electronics manufacturer Philips. It was such an event that the car was a specific model, called the Hillman 'Melody Minx', with a bonnet mascot in the shape of a human harp.

3 **First push-button radio – 1939**
America's Delco introduced the first multi-button radio tuner.

4 **First signal-seeking radio – 1947**
Delco innovated again, making it far easier to listen to the radio without constantly needing to adjust it.

5 **First FM radio receiver – 1952**
This was created and offered for sale by Germany's Blaupunkt.

6 **First all-transistor radio – 1955**
Solid-state radios, without valves, were finding their way into homes, while the first car versions were offered by Chrysler.

7 **First stereo radio – 1969**
Germany's Blaupunkt offered the first stereo-broadcast radio.

8 **First radio-cassette player – 1971**
After the cheap cassette player had been perfected by Motorola, Pontiac added one to its radios as an option.

9 **First motorcycle radio – 1980**
Japan's Clarion devised a set for two-wheelers, first fitted as standard by Honda.

10 **First digital car radio – 2002**
General Motors of Canada decided to fit digital-audio broadcasting-compatible radios – hitherto expensive gadgets – as standard to its Chevrolets.

10 inches that made history

Alec Issigonis, the maverick genius behind the original Mini, is supposed to have said to Tom French, Dunlop's chief designer: 'Give me wheels this size.' French took a ruler and measured the space between Issigonis's outstretched hands. It was 10 inches (25 cm). Whether true or not, Dunlop went on to make the specially sized wheels and tyres, unique to the Mini, as part of Issigonis's fastidious packaging requirements for the little car; they made for smaller wheel arches, which robbed less space from the interior. 'Ordinary' 12-inch (30-cm) tyres were standardized across the range in 1984.

Quite possibly the best car quote of all time ...

'Nothing handles better than a rented car.'
P.J. O'Rourke, satirist, 1987

... although these are very memorable, too

*'Father made the most popular car in the world.
I would like to make the best.'*
Edsel Ford, President of Ford Motor Company
[of the Lincoln Continental], 1939

*'Two generations of Americans really know more
about the Ford coil than the clitoris, about the
planetary system of gears than the solar system.'*
John Steinbeck, writer, 1945

'It'll turn on a sixpence – whatever that is.'
Nubar Gulbenkian, oil tycoon [of his custom-made London taxi], 1965

*'The [Porsche] 911 is almost too perfect:
agile, obedient, incredibly fast, yet some of its
character has been lost. It is like having a
conversation with someone on the phone.
With the [Porsche] 356, they're actually in the room.'*
Rt Hon. Alan Clark, MP, 1998

*'If pigs are big and popular, I guess
we'll make pigs.'*
Harry Pearce, Vice-president of General Motors [of SUVs], 2000

How did Jeep get its name?

The exact story is impossible to verify, but there are three theories about how the Jeep got its name, of which the third is the most likely:

(1) 'Jeep' was the simple slurring of the acronym GP, for General Purpose, by US Army personnel during World War II, as they became familiar with their new lightweight four-wheel-drive utility vehicle.

(2) The name was coined by Colonel E.W. Herrington of the US Army as far back as 1934 in Oklahoma, for a truck laden with oil-drilling equipment.

(3) The name was coined in 1940 by Sgt James T. O'Brien of the 109th Ordnance Company at Fort Ripley, Minnesota, for four- and six-wheel-drive vehicles under test that were made by the Minneapolis-Moline Power Implement Company. O'Brien is said to have named it after 'Eugene the Jeep', a popular newspaper cartoon character from the Popeye strip first drawn by E.C. Segar in 1936.

20 celebrity car deaths

If you're famous, a car-related death certainly builds your mystique, as these tragic endings prove.

Star	Scene	Date	Car
Marc Bolan	London, UK	16 Sept. 1977	driving his Mini 1275 GT
Albert Camus	near Paris, France	4 Jan. 1960	driving his Facel Vega
Eddie Cochran	Wiltshire, UK	17 April 1960	passenger in Ford Consul MkII taxi
James Dean	California, USA	30 Sept. 1955	driving his Porsche 550 Spyder
Brandon de Wilde	Colorado, USA	6 July 1972	driving unknown car
Princess Diana	Paris, France	31 Aug. 1997	passenger in Mercedes-Benz S280
Isadora Duncan	Nice, France	14 Sept. 1927	passenger in Amilcar
Grace Kelly	South of France	13 Sept. 1982	driving her Rover 3500S
John F. Kennedy	Texas, USA	22 Nov. 1963	shot in Lincoln Continental
Sam Kinison	California, USA	10 April 1992	driving his Pontiac Firebird
Desmond Llewellyn	East Sussex, UK	19 Dec. 1999	driving his Renault Mégane
Lisa Lopes	Honduras	25 April 2002	driving a Mitsubishi Montero
Jayne Mansfield	Mississippi, USA	29 June 1967	passenger in Buick Electra
Margaret Mitchell	Georgia, USA	11 Aug. 1949	hit by a taxi
Tom Mix	Arizona, USA	12 Oct. 1940	driving his Cord
Helmut Newton	California, USA	23 Jan. 2004	driving his Cadillac
Alan J. Pakula	New York, USA	19 Nov. 1998	driving his Volvo
Gen. George Patton	Heidelberg, Germany	21 Dec. 1945	passenger in Cadillac
Jackson Pollock	New York, USA	11 Aug. 1956	driving his Oldsmobile
Steve Prefontaine	Oregon, USA	30 May 1975	driving his MGB GT

The turbocharged keyboard

The world's most prolific author of car- and motoring-related books is Britain's Graham Robson, now in his seventies. Following stints in motorsport management, journalism and engineering, Robson co-wrote his first book, entitled *The Big Drive*, in 1970 while accompanying the World Cup Rally between London and Mexico. Since then, he has had 132 titles published – an average of one every three months – on an enormous variety of car topics, but with many concerning rallying. Robson has written more books on Ford than on any other marque.

Timeline of car safety innovations

We take the safety aspect of our vehicles for granted these days, but if it weren't for these key innovations, cars would be considerably more threatening to occupants and, increasingly, pedestrians, than they are.

1934 Barrier-impact test
General Motors was first to test the accident-resistance characteristics of its products by slamming them at low speeds into fixed objects. In those days the driver had to jump free at the last moment.

1939 Roll-over test
Auto Union, the precursor of today's Audi, was the first manufacturer to subject its cars to tests to see what happened when they barrel-rolled.

1948 Crumple zones
Preston Tucker's brave attempt to take on Detroit produced an advanced car: it was the first to feature crumple zones, plus a spring-loaded windscreen that popped out in a crash, rather than shattering *in situ*.

1949 Passenger safety cell
Saab's very first car, the 92, featured a structure that incorporated a strong, welded 'cage' to protect occupants in a crash – an idea inspired by the company's background in aircraft production.

1957 Front seatbelts
Volvo became the first carmaker to fit lap belts to the front seats as standard. Two years later, it replaced them with the much more effective three-point seatbelts.

1966 Anti-lock brakes
The first anti-skid braking system, known as Maxaret, was made by Dunlop and fitted to the Jensen FF. In a double first, the FF was also the first four-wheel-drive road car.

1967 Rear seatbelts
Volvo remained ahead of the game when it started fitting rear seatbelts. By 1972 its rear belts were three-point, too, and in 1999 the company was first to fit three-point seatbelts across all rear seats in every model.

1968 Head restraints
Volvo added head restraints to the standard specification of its cars, as it knew they enormously reduced chances of neck injury in an impact. Within a few years, American legislators obliged carmakers to fit them on all new cars.

1971 Traction control
Computer-regulated traction control monitored wheel-spin and modulated engine power for safer roadholding. The system, named MaxTrac, made its debut in Buick's full-size cars that year.

1972 Child locks
Volvo pioneered rear passenger doors that could be locked so they couldn't be opened from inside, for which every parent is eternally grateful. In 1972 the company fitted the locks to its 144 and 164 saloons and the 145 estate.

1973 Airbag *Illustrated below*
The development of the airbag was sparked by the US government in 1966: carmakers were ordered to devise car safety standards, particularly to protect unbelted occupants. The first car sold fitted with an optional airbag was an Oldsmobile Toronado.

1986 Seatbelt pre-tensioner
Audi pioneered the pre-tensioner and called it Procon 10. Triggered by high G forces involved in a collision, mechanical cables tightened the seatbelts to keep occupants upright, while pulling the steering wheel away from the driver.

1995 Electronic stability control
Designed to counteract errant car-handling characteristics, this system was pioneered by Germany's Robert Bosch, and first delivered to consumers on the Mercedes-Benz S-Class and BMW 7 Series.

1998 Adaptive cruise control
Mercedes-Benz broke new ground with its Distronic system. Using radar technology, the car could be slowed automatically to keep a safe distance from the vehicle in front.

2003 Lane departure warning system
A Honda Accord, sold only in Japan, was first with an 'autopilot' device, called the Honda Intelligent Driver Support system. The device governed the car's closing speed to the vehicle in front in order to keep a safe distance, and also kept the car within lane markings.

2006 Flip-up bonnet
Designed to cushion unfortunate pedestrians in the event of a frontal collision, the feature arrived on the 2006 model Citroën C6 and Jaguar XK.

10 top tips for safer winter motoring

If you really want to be prepared for the worst of winter weather, then make this your checklist:

1 Ensure your car is serviced in advance, with hoses and drive-belts in particular checked and replaced if necessary.

2 Check anti-freeze levels and top up if required.

3 Over-inflated tyres are especially dangerous on winter roads, so check the pressures when the car has been stationary for a period and the tyres are cold. They should be well above the minimum legal tread depth.

4 If you have an older car that you depend on, you might consider replacing the battery routinely, as you might in your mobile phone – say, every two years. Batteries have a finite life, even after topping-up and recharging.

5 Corrosion on battery terminals and connections is often the reason a car refuses to start, so it is prudent to clean them up and spray them with anti-corrosive penetrating oil.

6 Check that every bulb in lights is functioning properly, including in reversing and fog lights.

7 Inspect your windscreen-wiper blades for splits and replace them if there's the slightest evidence of any wear.

8 Ensure the windscreen-washer bottle is fully topped up with cold-weather screenwash fluid.

9 Clean the windows and windscreen before leaving home, but never use very hot water because it could crack the glass.

10 What's in your car for emergencies? Here are two lists, one for everyone who will experience a mild winter, and one for those who regularly endure a severe one:

In every car	Plus, for severe winters
windscreen de-icer	snow chains
ice-scraper	shovel
torch	warm clothes
road atlas	chocolate
screenwash	blanket
spare lightbulbs	boots with good grip
pad and pen	spare mobile-phone battery

'People's cars'

Putting an entire nation on wheels is quite some achievement. Henry Ford was the first to prove that it could be done with his Model T, and other countries slowly followed his lead, albeit with mostly very small and very cheap models. These are the notable 'people's cars' that laid the ground for today's mass car ownership worldwide:

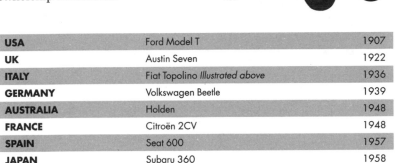

USA	Ford Model T	1907
UK	Austin Seven	1922
ITALY	Fiat Topolino *Illustrated above*	1936
GERMANY	Volkswagen Beetle	1939
AUSTRALIA	Holden	1948
FRANCE	Citroën 2CV	1948
SPAIN	Seat 600	1957
JAPAN	Subaru 360	1958
RUSSIA	Zaporozhets	1960
EAST GERMANY	Trabant P601	1962
INDIA	Maruti 800	1983

The numbers game: how your street lights boost global warming

In **five** countries, France, Germany, Belgium, the UK and the northern part of the United States ... in cities and towns with a population of **100,000** people ... there will be about **18,000** street lamps ... which will burn for an average of **4000** hours a year ... at an average wattage of **150** ... meaning that each city will consume **11 billion** watt hours of energy for street lighting ... alternatively known as **11 gigawatt hours** ... and that, as **one** kilowatt hour (1000 watt hours) of electricity produces an average of **340** grams of CO_2 ... the street lights of a typical Western town pump **3700** tons of CO_2 into the atmosphere annually.

The lives of the motor industry's founders

These 30 men, whose names still resonate – and matter – today, laid the foundation stones of the present-day car industry. For advice on how you could emulate them, see the bottom of the table.*

Giovanni Agnelli	founded Fiat in 1899, aged 33; died in 1945 aged 79
Herbert Austin	founded Austin in 1906, aged 40; died in 1947, aged 81
Walter Bentley	founded Bentley in 1919, aged 31; died in 1971, aged 83
Carl Benz	founded what became (in 1926) Mercedes-Benz in 1885, aged 41; died in 1929, aged 85
Ettore Bugatti	founded Bugatti in 1909, aged 28; died in 1947, aged 66
David Buick	founded Buick in 1903, aged 48; died in 1929, aged 74
Colin Chapman	founded Lotus in 1951, aged 23; died in 1982, aged 54
Walter Chrysler	founded Chrysler in 1924, aged 49; died in 1940, aged 65
André Citroën	founded Citroën in 1919, aged 41; died in 1935, aged 57
John Dodge	co-founded Dodge in 1914, aged 46; died in 1920, aged 52
Horace Dodge	co-founded Dodge in 1914, aged 42; died in 1920, aged 48
William Durant	founded General Motors in 1908, aged 47; died in 1947, aged 86
Enzo Ferrari	founded Ferrari in 1940, aged 42; died in 1989, aged 91
Henry Ford	founded Ford in 1903, aged 40; died in 1947, aged 84
Soichiro Honda	founded Honda (to make motorcycles) in 1946, aged 40; died in 1991, aged 85 *Illustrated right*
Cecil Kimber	founded MG in 1924, aged 36; died in 1945, aged 57

Frederick Lanchester	founded Lanchester in 1895, aged 27; died in 1946, aged 78
Vincenzo Lancia	founded Lancia in 1906, aged 25; died in 1937, aged 56
Henry Leland	founded Cadillac in 1902, aged 55; died in 1931, aged 84
William Lyons	founded Jaguar (as SS Cars) in 1931, aged 30; died in 1985, aged 84
Karl Maybach	founded Maybach in 1921, aged 42; died in 1960, aged 81
William Morris	founded Morris in 1913, aged 42; died in 1963, aged 92
Ransom Olds	founded Oldsmobile in 1896, aged 32; died in 1950, aged 86
Armand Peugeot	founded Peugeot in 1890, aged 41; died in 1915, aged 66
Ferdinand Porsche	founded Porsche in 1948, aged 73; died in 1951, aged 76
Louis Renault	founded Renault in 1899, aged 22; died in 1944, aged 67
Charles Rolls	co-founded Rolls-Royce in 1904, aged 27; died in 1910, aged 33
Henry Royce	co-founded Rolls-Royce in 1904, aged 41; died in 1933, aged 70
Eiji Toyoda	founded Toyota in 1936, aged 23; now 94
John Willys	founded Willys (later to introduce Jeep) in 1914, aged 41; died in 1935, aged 62

* If you want to found your own automotive empire, then you might be interested to know that the average age of these motor-industry greats when they founded their companies was 38.2 years. Louis Renault (the most youthful but the greatest of the Renault brothers) was the youngest, at 22, and Ferdinand Porsche the oldest, at 73 (although he had been a consultant engineer for many years previously). The average life expectancy is 72.5 years and (thanks to Eiji Toyoda, still alive at 94) growing. Charles Rolls died tragically young as the world's first air-crash fatality, while the stress of the Delorean affair is said to have done for Colin Chapman at 54.

The biggest development budget of all time

Some carmakers are cagier than others about revealing how much they spend on bringing an individual model to the market. Of those that do declare their budgets, Ford remains unsurpassed. In 1993 it spent £4 billion on its project codenamed 'CDW27', better known today as the first Ford Mondeo. The huge amount of cash went on ensuring that this 'world car' suited both European and American markets.

The lowest road cars ever

- Few cars have made such a virtue of their tiny height as Ford's GT40, a formidable sports-racing car that saw multiple Le Mans victories. The car's name refers to its 40-inch (100-cm) height (*illustrated below*).

- The experimental but fully roadgoing Adams Probe 15 show car is actually the lowest street-legal car ever. Built in 1970 and powered by a Hillman Imp engine, it stood just 29 inches (72.5 cm) off the ground; the only way in was through the glass roof.

- The lowered Mini was a weird 1960s fad: the Rob Walker Mini Sprint was 5 inches (12.5 cm) lower than the standard car – 1½ inches (3.75 cm) removed from below the waistline, 1½ inches (3.75 cm) from above it, and the rest achieved by lowered suspension.

- In 2006 British custom-car king Andy Saunders built a 'Flat Out' car – based on a Fiat 126 he bought for £240 – that is 20²/₃ inches (52 cm) tall. Its windscreen is 5³/₄ inches (14.75 cm) high and its engine 18²/₃ inches (47 cm) high. It travelled to Australia to feature in the 2007 Melbourne Motor Show, and is said to be fully drivable.

My Mother the Car: worst TV show of all time

The supernatural sitcom *My Mother the Car*, aired by NBC in 1965–66, is regularly lampooned as one of the most terrible TV shows ever. '*My Mother the Car* tried combining the US fascination with cars, sex and Mom', said a contemporary *Time* magazine report. 'But something happened in casting: Mother (who returns to earth from celestial regions, using the car radio as a voice box) is an invisible Ann Southern; and as for hero Jerry Van Dyke, he has finally answered the question: what is it that Jerry hasn't got that brother Dick has?' In 2002 *TV Guide* ranked only *The Jerry Springer Show* as worse.

Van Dyke plays lawyer Dave Crabtree, who sets out to buy a second-hand family car, and finds a 1928 Porter for sale. As he's inspecting it, his late mum's voice blurts out of the car radio: 'Hello, Davie. It's your mother!' Yes, she's been 'rein-car-nated' as an automobile, and the 30 weekly episodes – complete with canned laughter – followed Dave's family's exasperation with the old jalopy (only Dave can hear his mother's voice, putting his sanity into constant question) and the efforts of a sinister antique-car collector to get his hands on the Porter.

The show was created by Allan Burns and Chris Hayward, later behind the hit *Mary Tyler Moore Show*, and the theme song was released as a record by Jerry Van Dyke.

The 1928 'Porter' was entirely fictitious, and the two bright-red cars with white tops used for filming were created for the show by custom-car maestro George Barris. They had a Chevrolet V8 engine, automatic transmission, and body panels culled and modified from such diverse cars as Chevrolets, Ford Model Ts, Hudsons and Maxwells. Apparently invisibly propelled, the 'Porter' was controlled by a driver concealed inside the car, who manoeuvred it using mirrors. Both custom-built cars still exist.

The biggest car park in the world

The largest public car park in the world is the one adjoining the West Edmonton Mall shopping centre in Edmonton, Canada. It can take 20,000 vehicles and has 'overflow space' for 10,000 more for busy periods, such as the Christmas shopping rush.

Dictators' cars

Men who want everything their own way have often become national leaders who've made sure they got exactly the car they wanted as well:

Leonid Brezhnev – Rolls-Royce Silver Shadow

The hard-line Soviet leader was given an armoured Shadow as a present by US president Richard Nixon, but he crashed it into a truck during an official parade in Moscow in 1980.

General Francisco Franco – Rolls-Royce Phantom IV

Spain's military dictator ordered two colossal Phantom limousines in 1952, both meekly provided by Rolls and coachbuilder H.J. Mulliner.

Adolf Hitler – Mercedes-Benz 770K

The Führer's car was the biggest Merc available, at 19 feet (580 cm) long and over 7 feet (213 cm) wide, and was also bullet-proofed.

Benito Mussolini – Alfa Romeo 2900

The Italian Fascist leader competed in the 1936 Mille Miglia endurance road race in this car, 'co-driving' with his chauffeur to finish 13th overall and third in class. *Illustrated opposite.*

Benito Mussolini – Fiat 2800

In 1940 Il Duce bought one for his mistress, Clara Petacci. It had black Touring coachwork with red leather upholstery. Mussolini and Petacci were both shot dead in 1945 after attempting to flee the Allies in it.

President Josip Broz Tito – Cadillac Eldorado

The man who held together the six republics comprising Yugoslavia treated himself to a stretched 1960 Cadillac convertible for public appearances; ominously, the number plate sported the Red Star of Serbia.

Rafael Trujillo – Chrysler Crown Imperial

The 'father figure' of the Dominican Republic ordered this Imperial stretch from Italy's Ghia in the late 1950s. After he fled to exile in France with a large fortune, his son Leonidas Trujillo bought that Italian coachbuilding company in 1963 for $3 million, selling it again in 1967.

Royalty love their exotic motor cars, too:

The Aga Khan – Maserati 5000 GT

Only 32 5000 GTs were made, and the one built in 1962 for the Aga Khan was significant because its styling was later adopted for the first Quattroporte saloon. The Shah of Iran was among the other purchasers of the car.

King Faisal of Iraq – Rolls-Royce

The King and his son the Prince Regent were regular customers at the London factory of Hooper & Co., which produced for them a fleet of enormous black Rolls-Royce limos with sumptuous interiors.

King Farouk of Egypt – Daimler DB18

Modest alongside most of the motoring leviathans commissioned by African royalty, this late-1940s four-seater cabriolet was intended for personal use by the last king of Egypt.

The Shah of Iran – Bugatti Type 57

The French government gave this to the Shah as a wedding present in 1939.

The Shah of Iran – Lamborghini Miura SV

This is the very car that's now owned by actor Nicolas Cage.

The Shah of Iran – Rolls-Royce Camargue

The Iranian monarch was a keen Rolls collector throughout his 38-year reign, topping off a star-spangled collection in 1976 with the first left-hand-drive Camargue.

Members of the FIA

The FIA (Fédération Internationale de l'Automobile) is the non-governmental organization that looks out for the interests of drivers globally. Perhaps best known as the ruling body of motor sport – in particular, Formula One – through the FIA Foundation it uses its charitable status as an international association of motoring organizations to promote research into safety, environmental protection and automobile technology. It has 154 founding members, and they are:

AA Automobile Association (UK)

AAA American Automobile Association

AAA Australian Automobile Association

AAB Associação Automobilística do Brasil

AAC Automobile Association of Ceylon

AAEI Automobile Association of Eastern India

AAK Automobile Association of Kenya

AAM Automobile Association of Malaysia

AAP Automobile Association of Pakistan

AAS Automobile Association of Singapore

AASA Automobile Association of South Africa

AASI Automobile Association of Southern India

AAU Automobile Association of Uganda

AAUI Automobile Association of Upper India

AAZ Automobile Association of Zimbabwe

ACA Automòbil Club d'Andorra

ACA Automóvil Club Argentino

ACAR AvtoClub Assistance Rus (Russia)

ACB Automóvil Club Boliviano

ACB Automóvel Club do Brasil

ACC Automóvil Club de Colombia

ACCHI Automóvil Club de Chile

ACCR Autoklub Ceské Republiky

ACCR Automóvil Club de Costa Rica

ACCUS Automobile Competition Committee for the United States

ACES Automóvil Club de El Salvador

ACF Automobile Club de France

ACI Automobile Club d'Italia

ACL Automobile Club du Grand-Duché de Luxembourg

ACM Automóvil Club de México

ACM Automobil Club din Moldova

ACM Automobile Club de Monaco

ACMC China-Macau Autosports Club (Macau)

ACP Automóvel Club de Portugal

ACR Automobil Clubul Român (Romania)

ACS Automobile Club de Suisse (Switzerland)

ACS Automobile Club of Syria

ACU Automóvil Club del Uruguay

ADAC Allgemeiner Deutscher Automobil-Club (Germany)

AKK-Motorsport Finnish Automobile Sport Federation

AL Autoliitto (Finland)

AMA Asociación Mexicana Automovilística (Mexico)

AMSJ Auto-Moto Savez Jugoslavije (Yugoslavia)

AMSM Avto Moto Sojuz na Makedonija (Macedonia)

AMZS Avto-moto zveza Slovenije (Slovenia)

ANETA Automóvil Club del Ecuador

ANWB Koninklijke Nederlandse Toeristenbond ANWB (The Netherlands)

ASAI Asociación Automovilística de Touring y Deportes de Panamá

ASN Canada FIA

ATCE Automobile and Touring Club of Egypt

ATCL Automobile and Touring Club of Lebanon

ATCUAE Automobile and Touring Club for the United Arab Emirates

Automotosport Federation of the Republic of Kazakhstan

AvD Automobilclub von Deutschland (Germany)

BIHAMK Bosanskohercegovacki Auto-Moto Klub (Bosnia and Herzegovina)

BKA Belarusian Auto Moto Touring Club

BMF Bahrain Motor Federation

CAA Canadian Automobile Association

CAA Cyprus Automobile Association

CAKF Hrvatski Auto i Karting Savez (Croatia)

CAMS Confederation of Australian Motor Sport

CBA Confederação Brasiliera de Automobilismo

CCB Car Club do Brasil

CTAA Chinese Taipei Automobile Association

CTMSA Chinese Taipei Motor Sports Association

DASU Dansk Automobil Sports Union (Denmark)

DMSB Deutscher Motor Sport Bund (Germany)

EASU Estonian Autosport Union

ELPA Automobile and Touring Club of Greece

EuroRAP European Road Assessment Programme

FAA Automobile Federation of Armenia

FADECH Federación Chilena de Automovilismo Deportivo (Chile)

FASC Federation of Automobile Sports of the People's Republic of China

FDM Forenede Danske Motorejere (Denmark)

FFAC Fédération Française des Automobile-Clubs et des Usagers de la Route (France)

FFSA Fédération Française du Sport Automobile (France)

FIB Félag Íslenskra Bifreidaeigenda (Iceland)

FMSCI Federation of Motor Sports Clubs of India

FPAK Federação Portuguesa de Automobilismo e Karting

GAF Georgian Automobile Federation

HAK Hrvatski Autoklub (Croatia)

HKAA Hong Kong Automobile Association

IMI Ikatan Motor Indonesia

iRAP International Road Assessment Programme (UK)

JAA Jamaica Automobile Association

JAF Japan Automobile Federation

JMC Jamaican Motoring Club

KAA Korea Automobile Association

KAK Kungliga Automobil Klubben (Sweden)

KATC Kuwait Automobile and Touring Club

KMSF Motorsport Kenya

KNA Kongelig Norsk Automobilklub (Norway)

KNAC Koninklijke Nederlandsche Automobiel Club (The Netherlands)

KNAF Knac Nationale Autosport Federatie (The Netherlands)

LAF Latvijas Automobilu Federacija (Latvia)

LAMB Latvijas Automoto Biedriba (Latvia)

LASF Lithuanian Automobile Sport Federation

Continued from previous page

LIA Icelandic Motorsport Association

MAI Motorsports Association of India

MAK Magyar Autóklub (Hungary)

MEMSI Automobile and Touring Club of Israel

MNASZ Magyar Nemzeti Autósport Szövetség (Hungary)

Motorsport Safety Fund

MRF Motormännens Riksförbund (Sweden)

MSA Motor Sports Association (UK)

MSA Motorsport South Africa

MSNZ Motorsport New Zealand

NACT National Automobile Club of Tunisia

NAF Norges Automobil-Forbund (Norway)

NZAA New Zealand Automobile Association

OAA Oman Automobile Association

ÖAMTC Österreichischer Automobil-Motorrad- und Touring Club (Austria)

OMDAI Organización Mexicana del Deporte Automovilistico Internacional

PMA Philippine Motor Association

PZM Polski Zwiazek Motorowy (Poland)

QATC Qatar Automobile and Touring Club

QMMF Qatar Motor and Motorcycle Federation

RAAT Royal Automobile Association of Thailand

RAC Royal Automobile Club (UK)

RAC Foundation (UK)

RAC Motoring Services (UK)

RACB Royal Automobile Club de Belgique (Belgium)

RACC Reial Automòbil Club de Catalunya (Spain)

RACE Real Automóvil Club de España (Spain)

RACJ Royal Automobile Club of Jordan

RAF Russian Automobile Federation

RFAST Russian Federation of Autosport and Tourism

RFEDdeA Real Federación Española de Automovilismo (Spain)

RIAC Royal Irish Automobile Club

Road Safety Foundation (UK)

SAF Saudi Automobile Federation

SAMK Národný Automotoklub Slovenskej Republiky (Slovakia)

SAMS Slovak Association of Motor Sport

SATA Saudi Automobile and Touring Association

SATC Slovenský Autoturist Klub (Slovakia)

SBF Svenska Bilsportförbundet (Sweden)

SFI Foundation (USA)

SMSA Singapore Motor Sports Association

TAA Trinidad and Tobago Automobile Association

TACI Touring and Automobile Club of Iran

TACP Touring y Automóvil Club del Perú

TACPy Touring y Automóvil Club Paraguayo (Paraguay)

TACV Touring y Automóvil Club de Venezuela

TCB Touring Club Belgium

TCS Touring Club Suisse (Switzerland)

TOMSFED Turkish Automobile and Motorsports Federation

TTASA Trinidad and Tobago Automobile Sports Association

TTOK Türkiye Turing ve Otomobil Kurumu (Turkey)

UAB Union of Bulgarian Motorists

UAMK Ústrední Automotoklub (Czech Republic)

WIAA Western India Automobile Association

YCTA Yemen Club for Touring and Automobile

ZMSA Zambia Motor Sports Association

ZMSF Zimbabwe Motor Sports Federation

1958: the year of the classic taxicab

Nineteen fifty-eight was a seismic year in the cab world. It was when both the United States and Britain first saw the taxis that would become rolling icons of their most vibrant cities. Unlike in other capitals around the world, the Checker and the Austin were purpose-built for the job and, at least at the beginning, they were offered solely as working vehicles. Here's how they compare:

	New York	London
Cab	Checker A8	Austin FX4
No. of passengers	six	five
Engine size	3.7 litre	2.2 litre
No. of cylinders	six	four
Power	89 bhp	56 bhp
Transmission	manual (automatic optional)	automatic (manual optional)
Traditional colour	yellow	black
No. of headlights	four	two
Length	199½ in. (498.75 cm)	180½ in. (451.25 cm)
Wheelbase	120 in. (300 cm)	110½ in. (275.5 cm)
Where built	Kalamazoo, Michigan	Coventry, West Midlands
Final version made	1982	1997
Replaced?	no	yes, by TX-1
Music fame	'Big Yellow Taxi' (1970), by Joni Mitchell	'The London Cab Tape' (1971), by Frank Zappa
Cinema fame	*Taxi Driver* (1976), starring Robert De Niro	*The Servant* (1963), starring Dirk Bogarde
TV fame	*Taxi* (1978–83), sitcom	*The Knowledge* (1979), drama

BMW: politically incorrect or not?

In English, it's the 'Bavarian Motor Works', but the acronym with which everyone is most familiar is BMW, from the German Bayerische Motoren Werke. The initials are sometimes referred to as standing for 'Black Man's Wheels', which seems to have just as many affectionate connotations as stereotypical ones, and they can also stand for 'Black Man Working' – as in the 1995 book by Julia Hare *How to Find and Keep a BMW (Black Man Working)*, which has been described as 'the searchlight you need to make your way around in the tricky maze of the black male shortage'.

'Bob Marley and the Wailers' is also thought to be a politically incorrect interpretation, but in fact this can be directly attributed to the Jamaican reggae star himself. In one interview in 1977, he responded to criticism of his recent purchase of a new German saloon by saying: 'I have a BMW, but only because BMW stands for Bob Marley and the Wailers, and not because I need an expensive car.'

The origins of the Sunday driver

We all have a good idea of what a Sunday driver is, but the term was first coined in July 1925 in an article published in the *New Yorker* magazine. 'The Sunday painter', read the text, 'is to the art-artist what the Sunday driver is to the owner of the Hispano or Rolls-Royce.'

According to the *Oxford English Dictionary*, the next sighting of the phrase came in a piece in the 26 January 1942 edition of the *Baltimore Sun* newspaper. The report included the following sentence: 'Sunday drivers and sightseers accounted for more than 70 per cent of the cars on the Eastern Avenue.'

The Wankel-engined production car

In 1951 German engineer Dr Felix Wankel began developing his rotary engine that replaced conventional reciprocating pistons with a rotor in the combustion chamber, and dispensed with a crankshaft. The main benefits were exceptional mechanical smoothness and excellent power delivery; the main downside was much greater fuel consumption. Wankel first installed one of his engines in a prototype car at the NSU factory in 1957. Several production cars then went on to use similar power units, all of which are listed below. However, the fuel crisis of the mid-1970s made these thirsty, if silken, units unattractive to consumers, and since then, only Japan's Mazda has persisted in offering one. In 1991 its 787B sports-racing car won the Le Mans 24-Hour endurance race, the only Wankel rotary-engined car (indeed, the only non-piston-engined car) to do so. These are all the Wankel-engined production cars:

NSU Wankel Spider	1963–67	2375 built
Mazda 110S Cosmo	1967–72	1176 built
NSU Ro80	1967–77	37,204 built
Mazda R100	1968–73	95,891 built
Mazda R130 Luce	1969–72	39,273 built
Citroën M35	1970–71	267 built
Mazda RX-2	1970–78	225,688 built
Mazda RX-3	1971–78	285,887 built
Mazda RX-4	1972–77	213,988 built
Mazda REPU	1973–77	16,272 built (the world's only rotary pick-up; sold USA only)
Citroën GS Birotor	1974–75	847 built
Mazda Parkway	1974–76	44 built (the world's only rotary minibus)
Mazda Roadpacer AP	1975–77	800 built
Mazda RX-5 Cosmo	1975–81	104,519 built
Mazda 929L Legato	1977–81	unknown number built
Mazda RX-7 Mk1	1978–84	570,500 built
Mazda Luce/929	1981–86	unknown number built
Mazda Cosmo	1981–90	unknown number built
Mazda RX-7 Mk2	1985–89	197,180 built
Mazda Luce	1986–91	unknown number built
(Mazda) Eunos Cosmo	1990–95	8875 built
Mazda RX-7 Mk3	1993–2002	43,954 built
Mazda RX-8	2003 onwards	162,113 built to mid-2007

25 car insurance claims

These excuses have supposedly all been written on insurance-claim forms after road accidents.

1 'Going to work at 7 am this morning, I drove out of my drive straight into a bus. The bus was five minutes early.'

2 'I pulled into a lay-by with smoke coming from under the hood. I realized the car was on fire so took my dog and smothered it with a blanket.'

3 'Q: Could either driver have done anything to avoid the accident? A: Travelled by bus.'

4 'The claimant had collided with a cow. The questions and answers on the claim form were: Q: What warning was given by you? A: Horn. Q: What warning was given by the other party? A: Moo.'

5 'On approach to the traffic lights the car in front suddenly broke.'

6 'I didn't think the speed limit applied after midnight.'

7 'I pulled away from the side of the road, glanced at my mother-in-law and headed over the embankment.'

8 'I collided with a stationary truck coming the other way.'

9 'In an attempt to kill a fly, I drove into a telephone pole.'

10 'An invisible car came out of nowhere, struck my car and vanished.'

11 'The guy was all over the road. I had to swerve a number of times before I hit him.'

12 'I had been driving for 40 years when I fell asleep at the wheel and had an accident.'

13 'I told the police that I was not injured, but on removing my hat found that I had a fractured skull.'

14 'The pedestrian had no idea which way to run as I ran over him.'

15 'I saw a slow-moving, sad-faced old gentleman as he bounced off the roof of my car.'

16 'When I saw I could not avoid a collision, I stepped on the gas and crashed into the other car.'

17 'The accident happened when the right front door of a car came round the corner without giving a signal.'

18 'No one was to blame for the accident, but it would never have happened if the other driver had been alert.'

19 'I saw her look at me twice. She appeared to be making slow progress when we met on impact.'

20 'I started to slow down, but the traffic was more stationary than I thought.'

21 'The car in front hit the pedestrian, but he got up so I hit him again.'

22 'I started to turn, and it was at this point I noticed a camel and an elephant tethered at the verge. This distraction caused me to lose concentration and hit a bollard.'

23 'The accident was caused by me waving to the man I hit last week.'

24 'Windshield broke. Cause unknown. Probably Voodoo.'

25 'No witnesses would admit having seen the mishap until after it happened.'

The biggest car plant on earth

Volkswagen's Wolfsburg site in Germany is the largest car factory under one roof in the world, at 0.62 square miles (160 ha). The factory site itself also boasts 45 miles (72 km) of railway track to shift the 2700 cars it turns out every day, thanks to the efforts of 25,000 workers.

The 10 greatest taxi rides in the world

In 2007 the website Forbestraveller.com claimed that these were the most glorious city drives on Earth, and best seen from the rear seat of a local taxi:

BEIJING from the east side to the west side via Dongchang'an Jie.

BUENOS AIRES from Recoleta Cemetery to the Teatro Colón via Avenida Nueve de Julio.

HAVANA from the old city to the Hotel Nacionál via the Malecón.

HONG KONG from the airport to the city.

ICELAND from Reykjavik to the Blue Lagoon.

ISTANBUL from Taksim Square to the Blue Mosque.

LONDON from Marble Arch to the London Eye.

NEW YORK Fifth Avenue from Eighty-sixth Street to Washington Square.

PARIS from the Hôtel de Ville to the Arc de Triomphe.

VENICE from anywhere to anywhere.

The 10 most famous car mascots

A mascot was once the crowning glory for any majestic radiator grille. A few survive to this day, but what do all the famous examples actually signify?

Marque	What is it?	Significance
Austin (UK)	'Flying' capital A	Designed to mimic the winged 'B' on a more expensive Bentley.
Bentley (UK)	Capital 'B' with wings attached	Meant to imply speed; on pre-1931 cars, the wings jutted from the sides; after that, they flowed out behind.
Duesenberg (USA)	Art Deco-style streamlined wings	Supposed to invoke speed and flight.
Hispano Suiza (Spain/France)	Stork in flight	Honours a World War I pilot whose name was given to the Parisian street where the factory was based; his lucky motif was a stork.

Jaguar (UK)	Leaping Jaguar sculpture	Commissioned from artist F. Gordon Crosby to stop a car-accessories firm selling its own, crude version.
Lincoln (USA)	Four-pointed 'continental' star in an oblong	Remnant from a heraldic crest (historically meaningless) introduced by Lincoln in 1942.
Maybach (Germany)	Two intertwined capital 'M's in an arrow-head outline	Originally stood for Maybach-Motorenbau, but now stands for Maybach-Manufaktur. *Illustrated below.*
Mercedes-Benz (Germany)	Three-pointed star in a circle	Created in 1926, it combines Daimler's three-star logo (symbolizing the company's ability to produce engines suitable for air, land and sea use) and Benz's laurel-wreath emblem.
Rolls-Royce (UK)	'Flying lady' female sculpture	Commissioned from artist Charles Sykes so that owners had a tasteful alternative to aftermarket mascots then available; the model was Eleanor Thornton, secretary to John Montagu, a pioneer motorist.
Stutz (USA)	Figurehead of Egyptian sun god Ra	Inspired by the discovery of the tomb of Tutankhamun in 1922, and launched on a new model in 1926.

International distinguishing plates

The system of country codes, carried by cars outside their registered home territory, is called 'Distinguishing Signs of Vehicles in International Traffic'. It was formalized by the United Nations in 1949 in its Convention on Road Traffic. Each code must be notified to the UN Secretary General (for example, when a country changes its name). Following is a complete list of codes, which are supposed to be displayed on a white oval sticker or plate near the rear number plate:

Albania **AL**
Alderney **GBA**
Algeria **DZ**
Andorra **AND**
Argentina **RA**
Australia **AUS**
Austria **A**
Bahamas **BS**
Bahrain **BRN**
Bangladesh **BD**
Barbados **BDS**
Belarus **BY**
Belgium **B**
Belize **BH**
Benin **DY**
Bosnia and Herzegovina **BIH**
Botswana **BW**
Brazil **BR**
Brunei Darussalam **BRU**
Bulgaria **BG**
Cambodia **K**
Canada **CDN**
Central African Republic **RCA**
Chile **RCH**
China (Republic of) **RC**
Congo **RCB**
Costa Rica **CR**
Côte d'Ivoire (Ivory Coast) **CI**
Croatia **HR**
Cuba **C**
Cyprus **CY**
Czech Republic **CZ**

Democratic Republic of the Congo (Zaire) **ZRE**
Denmark **DK**
Dominican Republic **DOM**
Ecuador **EC**
Egypt **ET**
Estonia **EST**
Faroe Islands **FO**
Fiji **FJI**
Finland **FIN**
France **F**
The Gambia **WAG**
Georgia **GE**
Germany **D**
Ghana **GH**
Gibraltar **GBZ**
Greece **GR**
Grenada (Windward Islands) **WG**
Guatemala **GCA**
Guernsey **GBG**
Guyana **GUY**
Haiti **RH**
Holy See (equating to Vatican) **V**
Hungary **H**
Iceland **IS**
India **IND**
Indonesia **RI**
Iran (Islamic Republic of) **IR**
Ireland **IRL**
Isle of Man **GBM**
Israel **IL**
Italy **I**
Jamaica **JA**

Japan **J**
Jersey **GBJ**
Jordan (Hashemite Kingdom of) **HKJ**
Kazakhstan **KZ**
Kenya **EAK**
Kuwait **KWT**
Kyrgyzstan **KS**
Lao People's Democratic Republic (Laos) **LAO**
Latvia **LV**
Lebanon **RL**
Lesotho **LS**
Lithuania **LT**
Luxembourg **L**
Macedonia **MK**
Madagascar **RM**
Malawi **MW**
Malaysia **MAL**
Mali **RMM**
Malta **M**
Mauritius **MS**
Mexico **MEX**
Moldova **MD**
Monaco **MC**
Mongolia **MGL**
Montenegro **MNE**
Morocco **MA**
Myanmar **BUR**
Namibia **NAM**
The Netherlands **NL**
Netherlands Antilles **NA**
New Zealand **NZ**
Nicaragua **NIC**
Niger **RN**

Nigeria **WAN**	San Marino **RSM**	Thailand **T**
Norway **N**	Senegal **SN**	Togo **TG**
Pakistan **PK**	Serbia **SRB**	Trinidad and Tobago **TT**
Papua New Guinea **PNG**	Seychelles **SY**	Tunisia **TN**
Paraguay **PY**	Sierra Leone **WAL**	Turkey **TR**
Peru **PE**	Singapore **SGP**	Turkmenistan **TM**
Philippines **RP**	Slovakia **SK**	Uganda **EAU**
Poland **PL**	Slovenia **SLO**	Ukraine **UA**
Portugal **P**	South Africa **ZA**	United Kingdom **GB**
Republic of Korea **ROK**	Spain (including African	United States of America
Romania **RO**	localities and provinces) **E**	**USA**
Russian Federation **RUS**	Sri Lanka **CL**	Uruguay **ROU**
Rwanda **RWA**	Suriname **SME**	Uzbekistan **UZ**
St Lucia (Windward Islands)	Swaziland **SD**	Venezuela **YV**
WL	Sweden **S**	Yemen (former Aden) **ADN**
St Vincent and the	Switzerland **CH**	Zambia **RNR**
Grenadines (Windward	Syria **SYR**	Zanzibar **EAZ**
Islands) **WV**	Tajikistan **TJ**	Zimbabwe **ZW**
Samoa **WS**	Tanganyika **EAT**	

Not all countries adhere to the convention. The following don't have a notified plate at all, or use unknown ones: Angola, Antigua and Barbuda, Bhutan, Burkina Faso, Cape Verde, Comoros, Djibouti, Equatorial Guinea, Eritrea, Guinea-Bissau, Honduras, Maldives, Marshall Islands, Micronesia, North Korea, Oman, Palau, St Kitts and Nevis, São Tomé and Príncipe, Solomon Islands, United Arab Emirates and Vanuatu. However, the following countries are known to use these, unnotified, ones:

Afghanistan **AFG**	El Salvador **ES**	Mozambique **MOC**
Armenia **ARM**	Ethiopia **ETH**	Nauru **NAU**
Azerbaijan **AZ**	Gabon **GAB**	Nepal **NEP**
Bolivia **BOL**	Guinea **RG**	Panama **PA**
Burundi **RU**	Iraq **IRQ**	Qatar **QA**
Cameroon **CAM**	Liberia **LB**	Saudi Arabia **SA**
Chad **TCH or TD**	Libyan Arab Jamahiriya	Somalia **SO**
Colombia **CO**	**LAR**	Sudan **SUD**
Dominica (Windward	Liechtenstein **FL**	Vietnam **VN**
Islands) **WD**	Mauritania **RIM**	Virgin Islands **BVI**

In Canada and the United States, the ovals have not traditionally needed to be carried on cars from neighbouring countries. This has led to an industry of imitation plates for tourists, which have included MV for Martha's Vineyard, OBX for the Outer Banks area of North Carolina and KW for Key West, Florida.

Cars lost overboard

Cars are exported from their countries of manufacture on huge cargo vessels called pure car carriers (PCCs). Vehicles can be rolled on and off them. The first carrier, the *European Highway*, was built for 'K'-Line in Japan in 1973. It could carry 4200 cars. The largest PCC currently operating is the MV *Mignon*, which can carry 7200 cars. When these giants of the sea sink, the consequent losses can be enormous. The three largest car cargoes lost at sea have all occurred since 2002. Although no lives were lost among the crew, plenty of cars met a watery end.

Ship name	Cougar Ace	Tricolor	MV Hyundai 105
Size	55,328 tons	49,792 tons	40,772 tons
Built	1993	1987	1986
Owner	Mitsui OSK Lines	Wilhelmsen Lines	Eukor Car Carriers
Crew	23	24	23
Route	Japan–Canada & USA	Belgium–UK	Japan–UK & Germany
Date sunk	24 July 2006	14 December 2002	22 May 2004
Place sunk	230 miles (368 km) from Alaska	30 miles (48 km) from UK	5 miles (8 km) from Singapore
Reason	ballast imbalance	container ship collision	oil tanker collision
On board	4813 cars	2862 cars	4191 cars
Models	Mazda 3s (60%, new); Mazda CX-7 (30%, new); Private imports (10%, used)	Volvos (70%, new); Saabs (18%, new); BMWs (12%, new)	Hyundais/Kias (75%, new); Private imports (25%, used)
Net Value	$91 million	$45 million	$40 million

It could have been the kiss of death ...

Joseph L. Hudson founded his department-store empire in Detroit, Michigan, in 1881, but also put up the financial backing for a local car-making company that became known as the Hudson Motor Company. He had absolutely nothing to do with the cars themselves, apart from preventing the surname of their designer from appearing on the bonnet. His name was Howard Coffin.

Car wash: the United States leads the way

The car wash naturally originated in the United States, where mass car ownership first took hold. No wonder the country has shown a clean pair of heels to rivals in this industry ever since.

- The first-ever dedicated car wash was opened in Detroit in 1914 and was called The Automobile Laundry. Cars had to be pushed by hand around the circular building.

- In 1928 The Automobile Laundry built a drive-through tunnel, making it the first automated car wash. By 1945 there were 32 automated car washes across the USA.

- It seems that the first use of the term 'car wash' was in 1948 at the opening of the Minit-Man Car Wash in Detroit. *Popular Science* magazine noted how customers were agog at the facility's 'spectacular blower-drier'.

- Hanna Industries of Oregon became the world's largest manufacturer of automated car-wash systems after company founder Dan Hanna opened a chain of car washes called Rub-A-Dub. Hanna opened his first Japanese outlet in 1967.

- Hanna Industries invented the automatic wheel-cleaner and polish-and-wax application in 1975. It now has 29,000 installations in 90 countries; shareholders include media tycoon Roy Disney.

- *Car Wash* was the name of a 1976 hit comedy film set in an LA car wash and starring Richard Pryor; its disco theme song was an international hit for Rose Royce.

The smallest diesel production cars ever

In 1976 French microcar manufacturer Guy Duport persuaded the licensing authorities to allow companies such as his to fit larger diesel engines to the city cars (which could be driven without a car licence) they made. This was granted on environmental grounds, because the cars previously used just smoky 50-cc two-stroke moped engines. The 1977 Duport Caddy, with a 510-cc Lombardini twin-cylinder diesel power unit, then became the world's smallest diesel car. Since then other microcar makers have gone even smaller, with the Microcar Spid! of 1986 probably the smallest, at 273 cc. Then, in 1981, microcar manufacturer Erad offered a single-cylinder 290-cc diesel-engined car, claiming it had a world-record fuel consumption of 1919 mpg (680 km/l).

Cars by mail order

The arrival of the annual Sears mail-order catalogue was keenly anticipated by households throughout the United States in the 1950s. This heavyweight book, with page upon page of merchandise, promised to supply anything Americans could desire, no matter how obscure. So how about a car? Your wish was Sears's command: starting in 1952, you could fill in the coupon and send off for its very own in-house car, the egalitarian-sounding Allstate. What's more, as 'The Lowest Priced Full-Size Sedan on the US Market', it had a unique selling point. The car was guaranteed for 90 days, its Sears-branded tyres for 18 months and its Sears-branded battery for two years. You could choose your Allstate from the car-accessories section of the catalogue or alternatively order one at a Sears store.

The Allstate, however, was not all it appeared. It was built by the Kaiser-Frazer Corporation and, grille and badges apart, it was the Henry J. model (modestly named after the Mr Kaiser who founded the company). This was a slow-selling and cheaply finished 'compact' model that lasted for just four years from 1950 to 1954. And the Allstate didn't do much to help its sales. In 1952 just 1566 Allstates were ordered; the next year, a mere 797. After that, Sears abandoned car retailing altogether.

10 fashionable limited-edition cars

The temptation to put cars and fashion brands together has proved irresistible to both industries, although it is usually a carmaker-inspired move to breathe some new life and interest into a model that is perhaps showing its age. Here are 10 of the most interesting pairings:

Marque	Label	Car	Year	Number made
Aston Martin	Alfred Dunhill	DB7	2002	10
Cadillac	Gucci	Seville Gucci	1979	200
Fiat	Sisley	Panda 1000 Sisley	1987	627
Lamborghini	Versace	Murcielago LP640	2006	10
Land Rover	*Vogue* magazine	Range Rover 'In Vogue'	1981	700
Matra-Simca	Courrèges	Bagheera Courrèges	1974	661
Mazda	Jasper Conran	MX-5 Platinum	2000	500
Mercedes-Benz	Giorgio Armani	CLK500	2004	100
Rover	Paul Smith	Paul Smith Mini *Illustrated below*	1996	1800
Toyota	John Galliano	Paseo Galliano	1996	50

The timeline of headlights

Without headlights, night driving would be just too hazardous to contemplate. This is how they have developed:

1898	Gas-burning acetylene lights are first used.
1908	Electric headlamps are first offered as standard by Peerless.
1914	First headlight integrated into the front mudguard is introduced by Pierce-Arrow.
1924	Twin-filament headlamp is widely introduced, offering main and dipped beam.
1935	Flip-up headlights are offered by Cord.
1940	US government introduces a law that all headlamps on cars sold there must only be 7 inches (17.5 cm) wide, sealed-beam and circular; the law sticks for 43 years.
1954	Load-sensitive headlamp-levelling system is introduced by Cibié on the Panhard Dyna.
1961	First non-round 'styled' headlamp is introduced on the Ford Taunus 17 M (*illustrated below, centre*) and Citroën Ami 6.
1963	'Twilight Sentinel', the system by which headlamps automatically switch themselves on as night falls, is fitted to Cadillacs.
1967	Headlights concealed by sliding covers arrive on the Mercury Cougar.
1968	Swivelling headlights on the Citroën DS turn with the front wheels.
1971	First halogen-bulb headlights, made by Hella, are introduced on the Volkswagen Beetle. *Illustrated below, right.*
1971	First headlamp wash/wipe system is offered by Saab.
1986	DE (for Dreiachsiger Elliptischer) reflector headlamp makes its first appearance on the BMW 750iL. *Illustrated below, left.*
1991	BMW's 7 Series innovates again, this time pioneering high-intensity discharge 'xenon' headlights.
2007	First light-emitting diode (LED) headlights arrive on the Lexus LS 600h.

The world's top 10 drives

Travel website Expedia recommends these routes if you really want to enjoy your driving when on holiday. This selection won't disappoint, and it is advisable to build in plenty of extra time so you can admire the gorgeous scenery rather than just drive on through it.

1 Pacific Coast Highway, USA

Los Angeles to San Francisco, via the glamour of Rodeo Drive and the splendour of the Santa Ynez Mountains, and with the coastline constantly in sight.

2 Garden Route, South Africa

Takes in the dramatic stretch of shore between Mossel Bay and Nature's Valley, together with the vast Tsitsikamma Forest.

3 New England, USA

Autumn is the best time for this drive; especially wonderful is the glorious stretch along the Mohawk Trail through the Berkshires in Massachusetts and on into Vermont.

4 Great Ocean Road, Australia

In Australian terms, a short drive, at 125 miles (200 km), and not far from Melbourne. You'll see dense rainforest, perfect beaches and breathtaking rock formations.

5 Northern Lakes, Italy

Start at Lake Orta, in the foothills of the Alps, before skirting Maggiore, Como and Garda. You'll never want to drive to a shopping mall again.

6 San Juan Skyway, USA

A stunning 232-mile (371-km) circuit of the Rocky Mountains in Colorado. There are five passes to storm as the varied scenery of one of North America's most famous natural barriers keeps you open-mouthed.

7 Miami to Florida Keys, USA

Probably one of America's most scenic drives. Miami and Florida Keys are themselves exciting, but the sweep of the Everglades in between is awe-inspiring.

8 Grossglockner, Austria

The Grossglockner Road is the longest and most spectacular highway through the Alps, and its topography provides plenty of challenges for skilled drivers.

9 Furka and Grimsel Pass, Switzerland

You'll need a head for heights on this amazing Alpine route, which winds 610 feet (2000 m) up into the mountains to give astonishing views.

10 From Bolzano to Cortina d'Ampezzo, Italy

The Dolomites Road is the highlight of any visit to the mountain range. The route is 130 miles (210 km) long, up to 6000 feet (2000 m) high, and can be done in three hours – although two days allow comfortable time to explore at leisure.

Cars with six wheels

Cars with six wheels have long captured the imagination, with prototypes being built between 1903 and 1905 by De Dietrich and Borderel-Cail (both in France) and Pullman (United States). Marketing such cars, however, has defeated every manufacturer that has attempted it. Italy's specialist firm Covini launched its C6W Spider in 2002 and is the latest to have hit snags in putting its car on the market, with only one vehicle built in 2004. The C6W has four steered wheels at the front and two at the back, while power comes from a 443-bhp Audi V8 engine that is centrally mounted. A similar concept was tried in 1977 by British company Panther Westwinds, but the Panther Six roadster (*illustrated below*) had to be abandoned after just two were built because tyremaker Pirelli proved incapable of making the low-profile rubber that the car's four front wheels demanded.

Tyrrell's P34 six-wheeled Formula One car gained a lot of attention in the 1976 and 1977 seasons. Even though it managed to win the 1976 Swedish Grand Prix, it soon became uncompetitive. In 1983 F1 regulations restricted all cars to four wheels only.

One successful branch of six-wheeled motoring did emerge in the 1970s, however, when such British companies as Carmichael International offered conversions of Range Rovers that added an extra axle at the back; they found such diverse uses as fire tenders and hunting vehicles for Saudi Arabian birds-of-prey enthusiasts.

Motoring dynasties

Japanese manufacturers Toyota and Suzuki, and to a lesser degree Honda, still have large family shareholdings, as well as family members working for them, and, surprisingly, some huge carmaking firms are still controlled by their founding families:

Company	Family	Stake (%)
BMW	Quandt	46.6
Ferrari	Ferrari	10
Fiat	Agnelli	30
Ford	Ford	15* (40% of voting stock)
Morgan	Morgan	100
Peugeot	Peugeot	30.22 (44.94% of voting stock)
Pininfarina	Pininfarina	67
Porsche	Porsche/Piëch	50 (100% of voting stock)

* There are 1,797,252,972 common shares in Ford Motor Company. There are also 70,852,076 'B' shares; these can be owned only by Ford family members, but have four times the voting power of common shares, giving this stake the equivalent of around 15 per cent equity.

The right side of the law

None of these is a legal requirement for driving on UK roads:

Heater	No lawmaker forces one on you, or a rear-window demister.
Reversing light	Handy to avoid hitting the garage door, but not mandatory.
Seatbelts	You must wear a belt if there is one, but front belts became a new car requirement only in 1961; surviving classics from before then don't need them retro-fitted.
Spare tyre	You don't have to carry one by law, and the Ministry of Transport Test (MoT) doesn't cover it anyway.
Speedometer	No need for one ... just as long as you instinctively stick to speed limits.
Three mirrors	Any cars made after 1978 must have an interior mirror and one exterior mirror – the second exterior one is up to you.
Two fog lights	From 1978, one rear fog light had to be fitted to every new car, but not two.

International speed limits

China has recently changed its laws to bring some order to its teeming streets now that car ownership is rising fast. India is lagging some way behind: speed limits are not a matter of concern there and are rarely enforced. For the rest of the mainstream motoring world, however, keeping speed in check is part of everyday life on the road. These are the (mostly kilometre) speed limits in major car-owning countries:

Country	Town	Main roads	Motorway
ARGENTINA	40–60	80–110	100–130
AUSTRALIA	50–60	100–110	100–110
AUSTRIA	50	100	130–160
BELGIUM	50	90	120
BRAZIL	40–60	70–90	100–120
BULGARIA	50	90	100
CANADA	50	80–110	100–110
CHINA*	40–80	80–100	120
CROATIA	50	90–110	130
CYPRUS	50	80	100
CZECH REPUBLIC	50	90–130	130
DENMARK	50	80	110–130
ESTONIA	50	90	110
FINLAND	50	80–100	120
FRANCE	50	90–110	130
GERMANY	50	100+	unlimited
GREECE	50	90	120
HONG KONG	50	50–70	70–110
HUNGARY	50	90–110	130
ICELAND	50	90	n/a
IRELAND	50	80–100	120
ISRAEL	50	100	110
ITALY	50	80–110	130
JAPAN	40–60	50–60	80–100
LIECHTENSTEIN	50	80	80
LITHUANIA	50	70–90	110–130
LUXEMBOURG	50	90	130
MALAYSIA	40–60	70–90	110
MALTA	50	80	n/a
MEXICO	30–70	80–90	100–110
THE NETHERLANDS	50	80–100	80–120
NEW ZEALAND	50	100	100

NORWAY	50	80	90–100
POLAND	50–60	90–110	130
PORTUGAL	50	90–100	120
ROMANIA	50	90–100	130
RUSSIA	50	90–110	110
SERBIA	60	80–100	120
SINGAPORE	50	80–90	90
SLOVAKIA	60	90–130	130
SLOVENIA	50	90–100	130
SOUTH AFRICA	60	80–100	120
SPAIN	50	90–100	120
SWEDEN	50	70–110	110–120
SWITZERLAND	50	80–100	120
TAIWAN	40–60	50–80	100–110
TURKEY	50	90	120
UK	50 (30 mph)	95–110 (60–70 mph)	110 (70 mph)
USA	40–70 (25–45 mph)	90–120 (55–75 mph)	90–130 (55–80 mph)

* China has a nominal minimum speed limit nationally of 60 km/h.

Automobilia at auction

Collectors of car-related objects will go to great financial lengths to get what they want, as proven by these five auction results:

(1) Dinky Toys pre-war Series 28 toy delivery van, in Bentalls department-store livery; sold by Christie's in 1994 – £12,650 (world record for any Dinky Toy)

(2) Matchbox Mercedes-Benz 230SL toy car, in very rare green paint and original box; sold by Vectis Auctions in 2000 – £4000 (world record for any Matchbox toy)

(3) Carless Coalene glass petrol-pump globe; sold by Sotheby's in 1998 – £10,000 (world record for any petrol-pump globe)

(4) Cloth helmet worn by pre-war Mercedes-Benz Formula One driver Hermann Lang; sold by Christie's in 1999 – £16,675

(5) Bugatti wristwatch, made in the 1920s by Mido (*illustrated right*); sold by Bonhams & Brooks in 2001 – approx. £31,700 (299,000 French francs)

Championship race circuits of the world: how they look from the air

Barcelona, Spain

Bahrain

Brno, Czech Republic

Donington Park, UK

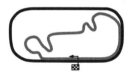

Hockenheim, Germany

Hungaroring, Hungary

Imola, San Marino

Indianapolis, USA

Interlagos, Brazil

Jerez, Spain

Le Mans, France

Magny-Cours, France

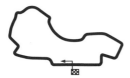

Melbourne, Australia

Monaco

Montreal, Canada

Monza, Italy

Nürburgring, Germany

Rockingham, UK

Sepang, Malaysia

Shanghai, China

Silverstone, UK

Spa-Francorchamps, Belgium

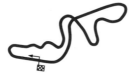

Suzuka, Japan

Turkey

Championship race circuits of the world: length v. speed

These circuits are all capable of hosting world-class motor-sport events, but no one has driven a car round them faster than these men. This is how long it took them to go the distance for each lap record:

Track	Length	Record lap	Driver
Barcelona	2.875 miles (4.627 km)	1 min. 15.6 sec. 2005	Giancarlo Fisichella
Bahrain	3.390 miles (5.411 km)	1 min. 30.25 sec. 2004	Michael Schumacher
Brno	3.350 miles (5.403 km)	1 min. 49.77 sec. 1988	Mauro Baldi
Donington Park	2.5 miles (4.023 km)	1 min. 18 sec. 1993	Ayrton Senna
Hockenheim	2.840 miles (4.574 km)	1 min. 13.78 sec. 2004	Kimi Räikkönen
Hungaroring	2.722 miles (4.381 km)	1 min. 19.07 sec. 2004	Michael Schumacher
Imola	3.063 miles (4.933 km)	1 min. 20.41 sec. 2004	Michael Schumacher
Indianapolis (F1)	2.604 miles (4.192 km)	1 min. 10.39 sec. 2004	Rubens Barrichello
Indianapolis (oval)	2.5 miles (4.023 km)	39.28 sec. 1992	Michael Andretti
Interlagos	2.675 miles (4.309 km)	1 min. 11.47 sec. 2004	Juan Pablo Montoya
Jerez	2.767 miles (4.428 km)	1 min. 15.65 sec. 1997	Michael Schumacher
Le Mans	8.476 miles (13.650 km)	3 min. 31.21 sec. 2006	Tom Kristensen
Magny-Cours	2.739 miles (4.411 km)	1 min. 15.37 sec. 2004	Michael Schumacher
Melbourne	3.293 miles (5.303 km)	1 min. 24.12 sec. 2004	Michael Schumacher
Monaco	2.074 miles (3.34 km)	1 min. 14.43 sec. 2004	Michael Schumacher
Montreal	2.708 miles (4.361 km)	1 min. 13.62 sec. 2004	Rubens Barrichello
Monza	3.597 miles (5.793 km)	1 min. 21.04 sec. 2004	Rubens Barrichello
Nürburgring	3.197 miles (5.148 km)	1 min. 29.46 sec. 2004	Michael Schumacher

Rockingham	1.479 miles	25.21 sec.	Jimmy Vasser
	(2.352 km)	2002	
Sepang	3.443 miles	1 min. 34.22 sec.	Juan Pablo Montoya
	(5.543 km)	2004	
Shanghai	3.387 miles	1 min. 32.23 sec.	Michael Schumacher
	(5.451 km)	2004	
Silverstone	3.192 miles	1 min. 18.73 sec.	Michael Schumacher
	(5.141 km)	2004	
Spa-Francorchamps	4.333 miles	1 min. 45.10 sec.	Kimi Räikkönen
	(6.976 km)	2004	
Suzuka	3.606 miles	1 min. 28.95 sec.	Michael Schumacher
	(5.807 km)	2005	
Turkey	3.318 miles	1 min. 24.77 sec.	Juan Pablo Montoya
	(5.34 km)	2005	

Let the train take the strain

The ability to load your car on a train in order to avoid exhausting long road journeys is something much valued by certain holidaymakers, although in recent years there has been a cut in the number of services offered (there are now none between France and Italy, and none in the UK). These are the remaining motorail services offered around the world:

Country	Service	Route(s)
AUSTRALIA	Indian Pacific	Sydney to Perth
AUSTRIA	Österreichische Bundesbahnen	Villach to Bulgaria (Plovdiv), Macedonia (Skopje), Greece (Thessaloniki) and Turkey (Edirne)
BELGIUM	Autotrein	Brussels to Bologna
CHILE	Autotren	Santiago to Temuco
FINLAND	VR	Helsinki to Lapland
FRANCE	Auto-Train (SNCF)	Calais/Lille to Avignon, Brive, Fréjus, Saint-Raphaël, Narbonne, Nice and Toulouse; Paris to Avignon, Biarritz, Bordeaux, Briançon, Brive, Fréjus, Saint-Raphaël, Geneva, Lyon, Marseille, Narbonne, Nice, Tarbes, Toulon and Toulouse
GERMANY	AutoZug (Deutsche Bahn)	16 German cities, including Cologne, Dortmund, Frankfurt and Munich to France, Italy, Austria and Croatia
ITALY	Trenitalia	Bologna to Palermo and Catania; Turin and Bolzano to Bari; Rome to Sicily (Palermo)
THE NETHERLANDS	Autoslaaptrein	s'Hertogenbosch to Bologna
USA	Auto Train (Amtrak)	Washington, D.C., to Sanford, Florida

Gerry Anderson's miniature star cars

TV producer Gerry Anderson has been described as the Walt Disney of UK TV, with a string of fondly remembered small-screen hits for children using (although not exclusively) puppetry and spectacular pint-size special effects. Cars have often been featured prominently.

Anderson's 1960 series *Supercar* had a car as its central character. Well, almost. The supercar in question, driven by hero Mike Mercury, didn't actually have any wheels, but could hover above the road surface, fly at high altitudes and dive into the sea. It was built by Anderson's right-hand man, Reg Hill, the model used for filming being 7 feet (2.1 m) long. The show was responsible for coining the term 'supercar', later used to describe exotic Ferraris and Lamborghinis.

The ever-popular *Thunderbirds,* first aired in 1965, featured a 7-foot-long (2.1 m) Rolls-Royce, with six wheels and the registration number FAB 1. This included a faithful replica of the majestic Rolls-Royce radiator grille after the British luxury carmaker gave its consent – but on condition that the scripts referred to it only as a Rolls-Royce (never a 'Rolls' or a 'Roller').

A rarely repeated Anderson show of 1969 is *The Secret Service*. Cancelled after just 13 episodes because it was felt to be too quirky for American TV viewers, it followed the adventures of a gadget-mad clergyman, Father Stanley Unwin, who worked undercover for the British intelligence service. The show intermixed puppets and real life, and Father Unwin drove a 1917 Ford Model T that existed as both a real car and an identical one-third-scale model 'powered' by remote control.

In 2005 Anderson's 1960s classic *Captain Scarlet and the Mysterons* was remade using only computer-generated animation – not a Lilliputian set or puppet was built. Captain Scarlet's car, the Cheetah, was created this time entirely on computers by Peter Stevens, one of the world's most famous car designers. He was careful to make it a feasible proposition as a full-size version, just in case it was needed for publicity reasons.

The curse of 'right-hand drive'

Global car design tends to originate with vehicles destined to be driven on the right-hand side of the road, *i.e.* cars with steering wheels mounted on the left-hand side. Then again, the car world is full of contradictions, such as:

- Volkswagen blamed mysterious 'technical reasons' for its inability to offer only a left-hand-drive Golf Mk1 GTi in 1977, but these were miraculously overcome and, after huge pressure from British buyers, a right-hand-drive version was launched two years later.

- The 1984 Bristol Beaufort convertible was offered as a left-hand-drive-only export model because its seatbelt mountings did not comply with British laws.

- Cadillac did not build a right-hand-drive car until 1915, and all Lancias until the 1950 Aurelia were offered as right-hand drive only (*illustrated below*, Lancia Lambda, driven by Greta Garbo). In Bugatti's early years, from 1909 until 1956, it never built a left-hand-drive model.

- Desirable BMWs have often come with the steering wheel on the 'wrong' side for such places as Britain and Australia: the 1973 2002 Turbo (Europe's first turbocharged road car), the first M3, the mid-engined M1 supercar and the Z1 roadster were all left-hand drive only.

- Road cars have rarely had a central driving position, except the 1993 McLaren F1, which had two passenger seats set back behind the driver. Modern fun cars inspired by historic single-seater racers, such as the Rocket and Brooke, also count. The 1937 Panhard Dynamic had a central steering wheel in the middle of a three-abreast bench seat, but it proved so unpopular that it was moved to the left two years later.

Rear-engined cars

At the dawn of the motor industry, several of the pioneering automobile designs featured a rear-mounted engine, although the pattern of front-mounted engine and rear-wheel drive rapidly became dominant. A few very light 'cyclecars' used a rear engine after World War I, but the concept was adopted by Dr Ferdinand Porsche for a series of prototypes in the early 1930s as a way to achieve aerodynamic design. One of these became the Volkswagen Beetle, which had a huge influence on other popular cars. By the 1970s, however, rear-mounted engines had become discredited because of the tail-heavy handling characteristics they exerted. Today the Porsche 911 is the only rear-engined production car of any note still on sale. This is a list of 100 rear-engined cars that entered mainstream motoring:

Abarth 500-1000	Fiat Nuova 500
AC Petite	Frisky
Alpine A110 Berlinette	Ginetta G15
Alpine A310	Goggomobil T300
Alpine A610	Goggomobil TS300
Amphicar	Gurgel Xavante
Autobianchi Bianchina	Hanomag
BMW 600	Heinkel Cabin Cruiser
BMW 700	Hillman Husky
BMW Isetta	Hillman Imp
Bond 875	Hino Contessa
Burney Streamline	Isotta Fraschini Monterosa
Chevrolet Corvair	Maico Champion
Clan Crusader	Mazda Carol
Coronet	Mazda R360
Delorean DMC-12	Mercedes-Benz 150S
Enfield 8000	Mercedes-Benz 170
Fairthorpe Atom	Messerschmitt KR175/200
Fiat 126	Messerschmitt Tiger TG500
Fiat 600	Mochet
Fiat 600 Multipla	Nobel
Fiat 850	NSU 1000

NSU 1200	**Skoda Estelle**
NSU Prinz	**Skoda Rapid**
NSU Wankel Spider	**Skoda S110R**
Opperman Unicar	**Steyr-Puch 650**
Peel Trident	**Subaru 360**
Porsche 356	**Sunbeam Imp**
Porsche 911	**Sunbeam Stiletto**
Powerdrive	**Suzuki Cervo**
Ramses	**Suzuki Fronte/SC100**
Renault 4CV	**Tatra 603**
Renault 8	**Tatra 613**
Renault 10	**Tatra T77**
Renault Caravelle	**Tatra T87**
Renault Dauphine *Illustrated opposite*	**Tatra T97**
Renault Floride	**Tatraplan**
Rodley	**Tourette**
Rovin D4	**Tucker Torpedo**
Russon	**Vespa 400**
Scootacar	**Vignale 850 Spider**
Seat 133	**Vignale Gamine**
Seat 600	**Volkswagen 181**
Seat 850	**Volkswagen 411**
Siata Spring	**Volkswagen 1500**
Simca 1000	**Volkswagen 1600**
Simca 1200 Coupé	**Volkswagen Beetle**
Singer Chamois	**Volkswagen Karmann-Ghia**
Skoda 100/110	**VW-Porsche 914/916**
Skoda 1000/1100MB	**Zaporozhets 965**

A warning of things to come

Modern cars today routinely come with a reflective warning triangle in the boot, ready to be erected near the car in the event of a breakdown in poor weather conditions. Such signs have been standard in German cars for years. The unlikely pioneer of this redoubtable safety aid, however, was Britain's all-but-forgotten Bond Equipe GT 4S, introduced in 1964. Its spare wheel was kept in a recess under the boot floor. When you lifted the cover off and looked on the back, there was a large red triangle painted on a white background. *Motor* magazine praised it in 1966 as 'a novel and intelligent safety device that other manufacturers might copy'. It was right.

The top 10 most ethical car brands

In 2004 the Ethical Consumer Research Association ranked car companies in order of their 'green' credentials. It rated them against 16 criteria, including environmental responsibility, safety and concern for human rights and animal welfare, and produced its table based on the manufacturers that attracted the least number of criticisms on these matters. The manufacturers were:

(joint) Peugeot
(joint) Citroën

Donated no money to politicians or lobby groups; focused on making small, thrifty cars; promoted biodiesel; issued environmental report on their own performances. No interests in the military or armaments.

Renault

Set its own, independently monitored targets for greenhouse-gas emissions, water consumption, waste and energy use; installed an innovative energy-saving Stop & Start system on some cars.

(joint) Volkswagen
(joint) Audi
(joint) Seat
(joint) Skoda

These four, all divisions of the Volkswagen group, were praised for research into alternative fuels, and for their environmental audit. Not singled out for criticism by any campaigning group; praised for trying to make their cars easy to recycle. On the employment front, 6 per cent of staff were disabled, and there was positive discrimination to boost female employment. No military links.

Honda

One of two marques making low-polluting hybrid cars; American car plants slashed emissions by 65 per cent in five years.

Honda also set energy-reduction targets for all areas of its operations. No military links.

Fiat

Decent employer, treating its workers well. Published environmental data for its plants; was working on alternative-fuel projects and aiming for a recyclable level of 82 per cent for its cars. No military interests.

 (joint) Kia
(joint) Hyundai

These Korean companies, parts of the same group, had respectable records on environmental awareness, and were focused on building small, fuel-efficient cars.

The 20 longest new cars you can buy

You can have any car 'stretched' to ridiculous lengths to create a limousine. The cars listed below, however, are the 20 longest standard production cars on offer today. (For comparison, the BMW 3 four-door saloon is 14 feet 9⁷/₈ inches /4520 mm long.) Interestingly, although the United States is often perceived as the home of the automotive behemoth, the leading nine cars in the league table come from other countries:

Car	Length
Mercedes-Benz S 600 Guard Pullman	20 ft 10¹/₈ in. (6356 mm)
Zil 41047	20 ft 9¹/₈ in. (6330 mm)
Maybach 62	20 ft 3³/₈ in. (6185 mm)
Bentley Mulliner	20 ft ³/₄ in. (6118 mm)
Rolls-Royce Phantom EWB	19 ft 11³/₄ in. (6090 mm)
Bentley Arnage limousine	19 ft 1⁷/₈ in. (5840 mm)
Rolls-Royce Phantom	19 ft 1³/₄ in. (5835 mm)
Zil 11041	18 ft 10³/₈ in. (5750 mm)
Maybach 57	18 fl 9¹/₂ in. (5728 mm)
Lincoln Navigator L	18 ft 7 in. (5671 mm)
Cadillac Escalade ESV	18 ft 6³/₄ in. (5660 mm)
GMC Yukon XL	18 ft 6¹/₂ in. (5648 mm)
Bentley Arnage RL	18 ft 6 in. (5640 mm)
Ford Expedition EL	18 ft 5¹/₄ in. (5621 mm)
Lincoln Town Car L	18 ft 5¹/₈ in. (5620 mm)
Hongqi CA7460 L1 Qijian	18 ft 4¹/₂ in. (5604 mm)
Chevrolet Suburban	18 ft 3¹/₄ in. (5570 mm)
Hongqi CA7460 L2 Qijian	18 ft 3¹/₄ in. (5569 mm)
Lincoln Town Car	17 ft 11¹/₄ in. (5470 mm)
Hongqi CA7460 L3 Qijian	17 ft 11¹/₄ in. (5469 mm)

The 11 laws of car creation

In 1995 *Autocar* magazine celebrated its 100th anniversary, making it one of the oldest motoring journals in continuous publication. The bumper centenary issue included a feature by its respected technical editor, Michael Scarlett, in which he saluted the 'creations' he rated as the most important in car design throughout the magazine's century. Here they are:

STRESSING THE BODY

MID-MOUNTED ENGINE

HYDROPNEUMATIC SUSPENSION

FOUR-STROKE (OTTO CYCLE) ENGINE

1959 BMC MINI [for its packaging] *Illustrated below*

PNEUMATIC TYRE

MODERN PETROL ENGINE

1903 MERCEDES 60 HP [the template for all mainstream cars until the mid-1960s]

MASS-PRODUCTION

AUTOMATIC GEARBOX

FOUR-VALVES-PER-CYLINDER ENGINE HEAD

The arrival of Maybach

Advertising statements don't get any bigger than Maybach's debut in New York in 2002. The enormous German car arrived in a glass case aboard the *Queen Elizabeth 2* cruise liner. It was then craned ashore and carried on a truck with a police escort to the city's Wall Street financial centre. Lunching brokers sitting out with their ties loosened in the July sunshine could only gape at the 18-foot (6-m) monster in an even longer tank.

Unique rear-light clusters

The vast majority of rear-light clusters found on cars have long been surprisingly similar – rectangles, squares or circles and, most recently, a wide variety of ultimately samey amorphous red plastic blobs. These 10 rear lights, however, have remained unique and highly distinctive:

1 BMW '02' series (early)		**6** Ford Mustang 1	
2 Cadillac DeVille		**7** Jaguar XJ-S	
3 Datsun Cherry F10		**8** Maserati 3200GT	
4 Fiat Brava		**9** Subaru Tribeca	
5 Ford Cortina Mk1		**10** Volvo S80	

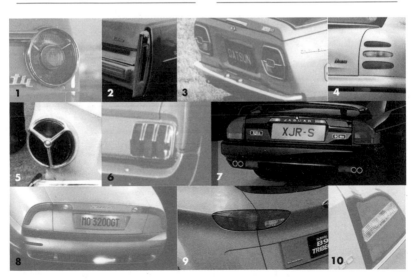

Van and pick-up versions of cars

The car-derived van or pick-up has been a fixture of the motoring scene since before World War II, and has usually been marketed with little ceremony. From the 1950s, however, manufacturers often chose to give their commercial vehicle variants an identity of their own – either to make them stand out or else to distance these workhorses from their more glamorous car cousins. This list of 40 car-and-van/pick-up siblings shows exactly what is based on what:

Original car	Commercial variant
Austin Metro	**Morris Metro** van
Bond Minicar	**Bond Ranger** van
Chevrolet Chevelle	**Chevrolet El Camino 2/3/4** pick-up
Chevrolet Impala	**Chevrolet El Camino 1** pick-up
Chevrolet Malibu	**Chevrolet El Camino 5** pick-up
Citroën Dyane	**Citroën Acadiane** van
Citroën Visa	**Citroën C15** van
Dodge Caravan	**Dodge Mini-Ram** van
Dodge Omni	**Dodge Rampage** pick-up
Fiat 127	**Fiat Fiorino** van
Fiat Palio	**Fiat Strada** pick-up
Fiat Uno	**Fiat Fiorino** van and pick-up
Ford Anglia 100E	**Ford Thames** van
Ford Anglia 105E	**Ford Thames** van
Ford Cortina 4	**Ford P100** pick-up
Ford Fairlane	**Ford Ranchero 1/3/4** pick-up
Ford Falcon	**Ford Ranchero 2** pick-up
Ford Fiesta	**Ford Courier** van
Ford LTD	**Ford Ranchero 5** pick-up
Ford Sierra	**Ford P100** pick-up
Hillman Husky	**Commer Cob** van
Holden Commodore	**Holden Crewman** pick-up
Jeep Cherokee	**Jeep Comanche** pick-up
MG ZR	**MG Express** van
Opel Corsa	**Opel Combo** van
Plymouth Horizon	**Plymouth Scamp** pick-up
Proton Wira	**Proton Jumbuck** pick-up
Reliant Regal	**Reliant Supervan** van
Rover 25	**Rover Commerce** van
Seat Ibiza	**Seat Inca** van and pick-up

Seat Panda	**Seat Terra** van
Simca 1100	**Dodge 1100** van and pick-up
Subaru Leone	**Subaru Brat** pick-up
Suzuki Alto	**Suzuki Mighty Boy** pick-up
	Illustrated opposite
Toyota Corona	**Toyota Tiara** van
Triumph Herald	**Triumph Courier** van
Vauxhall Astra	**Bedford Astramax** van
Vauxhall Chevette	**Bedford Chevanne** van
Vauxhall Viva	**Bedford HA/Beagle** van
Volkswagen Golf/Rabbit	**Volkswagen Caddy** pick-up

Turning circles

The turning circle, also known as the turning radius, is the distance a car covers in order to complete a circle with the steering at full lock. The turning circle gives a clear indication of how suited the car will be to crowded city streets. 'It's a measure of the car's maneuverability and how easy it is to park', says Gabriel Shenhar, a senior auto-test engineer for American magazine *Consumer Reports*. Thanks to its separate chassis design, the LTI TX1 'London' taxi has a turning circle of just 25 feet (7.6 m), while a typically sized medium saloon car, such as the Lexus IS200, has one of 33 feet 6 inches (10.2 m). The tiny Smart Fortwo turns in 28 feet 9 inches (8.75 m), while the gigantic Maybach 62 needs 48 feet 6 inches (14.8 m). Daihatsu claims a world-beating 22 feet 4 inches (6.8 m) for its four-seater Ai, although it is a concept car rather than a production model.

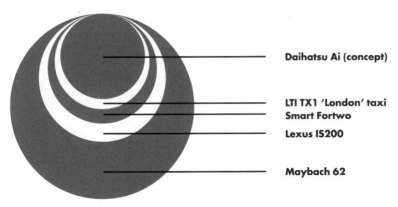

Daihatsu Ai (concept)

LTI TX1 'London' taxi
Smart Fortwo

Lexus IS200

Maybach 62

The crucial change in automatic transmission shift patterns

Ralph Nader, the safety campaigner and sometime presidential candidate, was instrumental in changing PNDLR to PRNDL. PNDLR was the mode pattern for such early automatic transmissions as the General Motors Hydramatic and the Packard Ultramatic, standing for (from top to bottom) 'Park', 'Neutral', 'Drive', 'Low (gear)' and 'Reverse'.

P
N
D
L
R

Nader highlighted how easy it was to drop from 'Low' to 'Reverse' accidentally and send the car careering out of control, with the possibility of running over people or hitting something. Ford was first in adopting Nader's preferred order, placing 'Reverse' on the other side of 'Neutral' to minimize the chance of an accident.

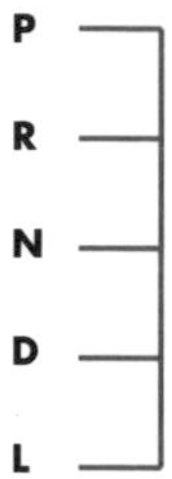

P
R
N
D
L

GM's Roto Hydramatic was the last automatic transmission to stay with the older style (until 1964), which by then included an extra speed. The S stood for 'Second'. Rivals, however, sported a safer automatic transmission shift pattern (*illustrated far right*):

P
N
D
S
L
R

P
R
N
D
S
L

20 facts about Hot Wheels toy cars

Forty years ago the American toy manufacturer Mattel introduced a line of tiny toy cars under the 'Hot Wheels' brand, and they're still very much with us today. Here are the essential facts behind these perennial pocket favourites:

1 Hot Wheels first came on to the market in 1968, although some models have '1967' stamped underneath.

2 The models initially cost 59 cents each.

3 The scale is supposed to be 1:64, at a maximum length of 3 inches (7.6 cm), although it has often been altered to suit the packaging.

4 The models' free-running axles and hollow, tapered plastic wheels made them faster than Britain's Matchbox 1-75 Series models, which they eventually put out of business.

5 From 1968 until 1977, Hot Wheels featured 'red line' wheels, with a red line on the tyre wall.

6 Between 1968 and 1972, the cars were available in 14 shades of mirror-like 'Spectraflame' paint.

7 Between 1981 and 1986, Hot Wheels 'Real Riders' were available, with tyres made from real Goodyear rubber instead of plastic wheels.

8 Hot Wheels are today made in India, Malaysia, China and Thailand. In the past they have been made in the United States, Hong Kong and Mexico.

9 Hot Wheels blister cards have been printed in English, French, German, Italian, Japanese and Spanish.

10 The first promotional Hot Wheels was produced as a giveaway for the American fast-food chain Jack in the Box; the first promotional example for sale was produced exclusively for Toys R Us.

11 In 1989 Ralston Purina made a Hot Wheels breakfast cereal.

12 The first Hot Wheels motorcycle was introduced in 1975.

13 Annual production of each single model is usually between 250,000 and 300,000.

14 Some popular models are in production for up to 10 years.

15 Collectors will pay a $2 premium for 'error' Hot Wheels cars with such flaws as mismatched wheels or a missing part, but they won't pay extra for a vehicle in the wrong blister pack.

16 Chevrolet Corvettes are consistently among the bestselling Hot Wheels; the 1968 Corvette, a tiny copy of the real thing, hit toyshops as a Hot Wheels car before the genuine article arrived in Chevrolet showrooms that year.

17 An estimated six Hot Wheels cars are sold every second worldwide – that's 518,400 a day.

18 Some 41 million American adults have grown up playing with Hot Wheels cars. Serious collectors are estimated to own an average of 1500 each, although North American children aged between three and 10 own an average of 24 each.

19 The highest price paid by a collector for a Hot Wheels car is thought to be $72,000, for the Beach Bomb, in rare pink livery. The bible for collectors is *Tomart's Price Guide to Hot Wheels*, now in its sell-out third edition.

20 Since 1968 Mattel has produced more than 2 billion Hot Wheels models, of more than 1000 different vehicles.

An A–Z of hot-rod slang

Hot rods are cars that have been modified to improve appearance or performance, or both. With this easy reference to hand, you need never feel out of your depth again when admiring someone's hot-rod pride and joy.

A

A-bone Model A Ford.
Appletons wing-mounted spotlights, named for the manufacturer.

B

baby moons small, chromed hubcaps that cover only the centre of the wheel.
balonies wide tyres, usually on the rear.
bang shift to shift quickly a standard transmission.
beast an ugly hot rod.
belly pan metal sheeting underneath a street rod, for streamlining.
billet aluminium aftermarket trim parts.
binders brakes.
blown gasser a supercharged, gas-burning engine.
bobbed shortened wings.
bucket a hot rod with a Ford Model T body.
bull nose a chrome trim piece for the top of a bonnet.
bullets chromed, bullet-shaped extensions used on bumpers, grilles and wheels.

C

cammer a single, overhead-valve Ford V8 engine.
Carson top a solid, removable roof covered with a soft material.
channel to cut the floor so that the body rests around the chassis rails rather than on top of the frame.
chop to remove a section of the roofline

horizontally to reduce its height (also called 'hammer').
continental kit an area used to store the spare tyre other than in the boot or undercarriage.
coupé any car with only front seats.
crate engine a factory-built, ready-to-run engine.
cruise to drive in a laid-back style.
custom a car modified to create a visually distinctive vehicle.

D

deck to remove the chrome and handles from the boot lid.
Deuce 1932 Ford.
dig out to accelerate quickly.
digger a dragster.
digs drag races.
dog-dish hubcap a small moon.
drop axle a front axle with a sharp downward bend as it leaves the wheel so it's lower than usual.
dropped a significantly lowered vehicle.
Dutchman panel metal body panel situated between the rear window and boot.
Duval windshield a split, V-shaped, raked, chrome-plated windscreen, designed by George DuVall.

E

elephant a 1964 or later Chrysler with a hemispherical-head V8 engine.
ET elapsed time – the time it takes to cover a quarter-mile drag.

F

fade-aways wings tapering back into the body.

fat an over-rich fuel mixture signalled by excessive black smoke.

fat fender a Ford built between 1935 and 1948 that is wide and rounded in appearance.

filled roof one with a welded steel panel instead of the original wood-and-fabric insert.

five-window a coupé body with five windows, not counting the windscreen.

flame-thrower a device used to ignite unburned exhaust gases.

flamed fiery body graphics starting at the front and working backwards on a hot rod.

four banger a four-cylinder engine.

four barrel a four-cylinder engine or type of carburettor.

four-on-the-floor a floor-mounted gearshift coupled to a four-speed transmission.

French to recess the headlights and remove the seam of the headlight trim ring.

G

gasser a modified closed car that competes at drag races.

ghost flames painted flames, the same colour as the body but a little lighter or darker.

glass-packs loud, aftermarket exhaust silencers.

grocery-getter a mild street rod used for shopping.

H

hammer *see* chop.

handler a hot rod that's easy to drive.

haze the hides to spin and smoke the rear tyres.

header a fine-tuned exhaust manifold,

usually chromed or coated.

hemi a high-performance Chrysler engine with hemispherical cylinder heads.

hides tyres.

highboy a hot rod with no wings or running boards and a high-mounted body.

huffer a supercharger.

I

in the weeds a really low car.

J

jug a carburettor.

juice fuel, electricity or hydraulic fluid.

K

kemp a hot rod with a customized body.

L

lakepipes side-exit exhaust pipes located under the rocker panels.

Lakes the dry salt lakes in and around Southern California where hot-rodders race their cars.

Lakes-modified a modified racer for racing at the Lakes.

leadsled a lowered, late-1940s car with moulded body seams, traditionally done with lead.

lean it out to alter the fuel/air mixture to improve engine performance and use less fuel.

locker a differential that helps prevent tyrespin and evenly distributes the engine's torque to the rear wheels.

loud pedal accelerator.

Louie a left-hand turn.

lowboy a hot rod without wings or running boards that has been lowered over the frame.

lowrider a car lowered by a hydraulic suspension system that can bring the ride height up in order to drive it.

Continued from previous page

M

mill engine.

moon a flat aluminum wheel cover.

moulded filled and reshaped body panels and seams.

mouse motor a small-block Chevrolet V8 engine.

N

nail-head a 1950s Buick engine.

nerf bars tubular bumpers used to ward off tyres in open-wheel racing cars.

newstalgia a hot-rod style that mimics the 1950s and 1960s but with modern components.

NOS nitrous-oxide system, for added power.

nosed chrome details and trim removed from the bonnet and smoothed over.

O

overwind to rev an engine beyond its limits.

P

pancaked a bonnet modified for a lower profile.

panel delivery an early commercial vehicle with two doors in the front for people and two at the rear for cargo.

peaked a moulded accent seam on a bonnet.

pearl paintwork reflecting mother-of-pearl iridescent colours.

phaeton an open two- or four-door sedan without wind-up windows, manufactured in the 1920s or 1930s.

phone booth a 1928/29 Ford Model A closed-cab pick-up.

pie-crust sidewall the sidewall scallops,

as seen on many of Firestone's bias-ply tyres.

pinch to narrow the front chassis frame to match the grille shell.

pinstripes long, narrow, painted stripes running the length of a hot rod.

pit pins quick-release pins holding body panels in place.

power-parker a hot-rodder who arrives as early as possible at shows to get prime parking spots.

pro-street a hot rod made to look like a drag-racer.

puffer a supercharger.

Q

quick change a rear end that permits rapid changing of gear ratios to suit the event.

R

rails the chassis-frame side rails.

raked a hot rod lowered in the front or raised in the back.

rat a 'big block' Chevrolet V8 engine.

reacher a dependable street rod.

resto-rod an original-looking car with a modified chassis or powerplant.

roadster a two-seater phaeton with a removable top, no wind-up side windows and a folding windscreen.

rod short for hot rod.

roll pan a smoothed-out panel replacing the bumper.

rolled and pleated a deluxe interior sewn with padded pleats.

roller a chassis complete enough to be rolled around on its own.

Roscoe a right-hand turn.

rubber rake a rake achieved by using big tyres at the back and little ones at the front.

S

sano short for 'sanitary', a hot rod that's absolutely spotless.

scatter shield a protective enclosure at the rear of the engine to protect the driver in case the clutch explodes.

section to remove a band of metal from around the middle section of a vehicle to reduce overall height.

shave to remove and smooth over door handles and body trim.

skins tyres.

skirts short for wing skirts, which cover wheel-arch openings.

slammed a hot rod as close to the ground as possible.

sleeper a car that doesn't look as fast as it is.

smoothy a hot rod with all raised portions of the body removed.

split window a rear window with two panes of glass.

stance the way in which the tyres and wheels cause the car to sit on the road.

steelies steel wheels.

step plates pads mounted on running boards or wings to protect paintwork or rubber matting.

stickshift a floor-mounted gearshift lever.

stone a slow car.

stovebolt a hot rod powered by a Chevrolet in-line six-cylinder engine.

street machine a street-legal, highly modified car or truck built in or after 1949.

street rod a street-legal highly modified car or truck built in or before 1948.

stroker an engine with an unusually long crankshaft throw with elongated connecting rods.

stuffer a supercharger.

T

T-bucket a short, wingless, open Ford Model T hot-rod body.

three-on-the-tree a column-mounted, three-speed transmission shifter.

trad rad a street rod built in the style of the 1950s and 1960s rods.

trailer queen a derogatory term for a rarely driven car.

tub to enlarge the size of the wheel arch to accommodate very large tyres.

tunnel like French, only deeper.

U

uncorked running without exhaust silencers.

V

Victoria a sporty two-door sedan body with distinctive rear panelwork.

W

wedge a Chrysler engine with wedge-shaped combustion chambers in the heads.

wheelie bars rods extending from the back of a car and connected to the wheels to stop it from flipping backwards during sudden acceleration.

wide weenies large rear tyres.

wide whites wide whitewall tyres.

wires spoked wire wheels.

X

X-member the centre portion of a chassis, where the frame rails meet or cross.

Y

Y-block a cylinder block with deep pan rails.

Z

Z'ed chassis rails altered to a Z-shape in order to lower the front of a hot rod.

zoomy a wild street rod with open exhaust pipes.

The 10 most influential people in the genesis of the car

There have been many key figures in the history of the car over the last 120-plus years. In their own ways, however, these individuals have done more than most to influence the car as we know it today:

1 Carl Benz (1844–1929)

The first man to design anything you could actually call a car.

2 Frederick Lanchester (1868–1946)

Britain's Lanchester devised interchangeable components and smooth-riding suspension systems, and took out more than 400 patents.

3 Henry Ford (1863–1947)

Mass-production advocate who sold 15 million Model Ts (mostly in black, as black paint dried quickest).

4 Edward Budd (1870–1946)

Ingenious American metalworker who pioneered the use of welded steel for mass-produced car bodies.

5 Harley Earl (1893–1969)

Hired in 1926 by General Motors after running his own customizing shop, Earl subsequently invented 'car styling'.

6 Ferdinand Porsche (1875–1951)

The father of the Volkswagen Beetle, the bestselling car ever, used similar technology to produce Porsche sports cars.

7 Sir William Lyons (1901–1985)

Neither industrialist nor engineer, Lyons had such an extraordinary grasp of 'brand values' that he created Jaguar from scratch.

3 Henry Ford

5 Harley Earl

6 Ferdinand Porsche

8   Sir Alec Issigonis (1906–1988)

The engineer whose doggedness created the Mini for the British Motor Corporation; it became the packaging model for all modern cars.

9   Eiji Toyota (born 1913)

Toyota's family made textile looms and branched into cars, rightly deciding that satisfied customers mattered most.

10 Ralph Nader (born 1934)

American consumer champion who lobbied successfully for mandatory safety features, including seatbelts and laminated windscreens.

7 Sir William Lyons

8 Sir Alec Issigonis

10 Ralph Nader

A poet's take on the Edsel

When Ford launched a brand-new line of cars in 1958, it decided to call them Edsel after Edsel Ford, son of the company founder, Henry Ford. But this was only after it had investigated several other avenues, one of which included consulting the American poet Marianne Moore, who, it was felt, would understand the nature of words far better than Detroit motor-industry executives. Moore's list of suggestions, submitted in 1955, included these madcap monikers:

ANDANTE CON MOTO	**SILVER SWORD**
CHAPARRAL	**THUNDERCREST**
INTELLIGENT WHALE	**THUNDERCRESTER**
MONGOOSE CIVIQUE	**TURCOTINGA**
PASTELOGRAM	**UTOPIAN TURTLETOP**
RESILIENT BULLIT	**VARSITY STROKE**

Approach, departure and breakover angles

These angles are important factors in determining a car's ability to tackle rough terrain, and are especially critical for 4×4 off-road vehicles:

- The approach angle, when seen from the side, is that between level ground and a line drawn from the front tyre to the lowest hanging point of the car's structure directly in front of it – usually the front bumper. It shows how the car can approach an incline and tackle obstacles without getting stuck or damaged.

- The departure angle is the mirror image at the back of the car. Viewed from the side, this is the angle between level ground and a line drawn from the rear tyre to the lowest point of the rear structure, such as a bumper or towing bracket. It shows how the car can leave an incline without getting snagged or damaged.

These are 25 representative sport utility vehicles (SUVs) and their approach/departure angles, measured in degrees, with the most go-anywhere at the top:

Hummer H1	72/37
Land Rover 90	47/47
Land Rover 110	49/35
Jeep Wrangler (current)	44/40
Hummer H3	37.5/37.5
Daihatsu Terios Mk2	38/37
Jeep Cherokee	38/31
Jeep Grand Cherokee	37/29
Toyota 4Runner	36/29
Mitsubishi Montero/Pajero/Shogun (two-door)	42/20
Isuzu Trooper	31/31
Nissan Pathfinder	30/28
Isuzu Rodeo/Opel-Vauxhall Frontera	32/24
Land Rover Discovery Mk2	31/25
Mercedes-Benz M-Class	29/26

Mitsubishi Montero/Pajero/Shogun Sport (four-door)	34/20
Honda Passport	30/24
Dodge Durango	28/26
Porsche Cayenne	29/25
Volvo XC90	28/25
Lexus RX300	28/23
Infiniti FX45	29/21
Ford Explorer (four-door)	26/18
GMC Jimmy/Chevrolet Blazer (four-door)	25/19
Oldsmobile Bravada	26/14

- The breakover, or traverse, angle is a measure of a car's ability to cross protruding obstacles without scraping, catching or damaging the underside. The 'included' angle is that within the raised incline; the 'excluded' angle (typically 20 degrees on an SUV) is that from the included angle to the car's lowest underside point.

Why cars in France had yellow headlights

It has often been suggested there's a scientific reason why cars in France had yellow headlights – something to do with yellow being less dazzling than white. Even a spokesperson for light-maker Cibié offered this story as an explanation. However, the truth is that, in 1938–39, the French government was already anxious about the growing threat of a German invasion. It decreed that all new cars should be fitted with yellow headlamp bulbs, and that existing cars should either have yellow-coated covers fitted on their headlights or have the clear glass replaced by a yellow-tinted one, so it would be easy to distinguish German vehicles at night and shoot at them. France, of course, was invaded, so the

ruse didn't help much, but the yellow lights rule stuck. Indeed, it was only on 1 January 1993 that France was made to follow European Commission Directive no. 91/663 on vehicle-type approval, forcing the country to step into line with other European countries. Today all new cars in France have white headlights, even though yellow fog lights did linger on patriotically on such cars as the 1991 Renault Clio 16V.

Toyota Prius: the green choice of celebrities

The Toyota Prius has become the celebrity car of choice in Hollywood on account of its 'green' credentials. What it lacks in typical Beverly Hills glamour it more than makes up for in environmental friendliness, thanks to its hybrid drive system. The Prius has a small traditional petrol engine yoked to an electric motor and a battery pack that is recharged using spare energy generated when the car is braking; a computer then decides if it's more efficient to use petrol or electric power, with the result that the unassuming saloon offers 68 mpg (4 l/100 km) – requiring half as many fill-ups as a typical American saloon equivalent. At rest, for example in traffic, neither power unit is used, which helps make the car super-economical and, therefore, kinder on the environment. Celebrities love that, and many run one as their everyday car in the Golden State. They include:

Jessica Alba	Kirsten Dunst	Donny Osmond
Jennifer Aniston	Will Ferrell	Gwyneth Paltrow
Jerry Bruckheimer	Harrison Ford	Brad Pitt
Chevy Chase	Jeff Goldblum	Natalie Portman
Brian Cox	Tom Hanks	Rob Reiner
Sheryl Crow	Arianna Huffington	Tim Robbins
Billy Crystal	Scarlett Johansson	Meryl Streep
Ted Danson	Angelina Jolie	Charlize Theron
Larry David	Jeffrey Katzenburg	Robin Williams
Cameron Diaz	Jennifer Lopez	
Leonardo DiCaprio	Ewan McGregor	

The Golden Zebra

In 1955 the Daimler 'Golden Zebra' was the world's most outrageous car. Its dazzling ivory paintwork, all-gold-plated trim, real ivory interior trim and seats covered in real zebra skin dazzled and appalled the public in equal measure. It began the trend for four-wheeled 'bling' long before anyone could imagine stretched Hummers, although the influence was more Alma Cogan than P. Diddy. The car was created by Lady Norah Docker, a Daimler director notorious for her lavish tastes, and included a vanity case, manicure set, cocktail cabinet and a concealed, telescopic umbrella. When asked why she chose real zebra skin for the upholstery, Lady Norah replied: 'Because mink is too hot to sit on.'

The basis of the car was a Daimler DK400 rolling chassis. Its bodywork and interior were created by craftsmen at the Hooper coachworks in west London, at a cost of £12,000 (then four times the price of a large house). Lady Norah and her husband, Sir Bernard Docker, Daimler chairman, used the car for their grand entrance at the wedding of Grace Kelly and Prince Rainier of Monaco in 1956. Shortly after it was completed, however, the Dockers were fired from Daimler for wasting money. The 'Golden Zebra' was the last of five* special cars, ostensibly built for promotional purposes, that became known as the 'Docker Daimlers'. They were:

- **1951 – 'Gold Car', based on a Daimler DE36**
- **1952 – 'Blue Clover', based on a Daimler DE36**
- **1953 – 'Silver Flash', based on a Daimler Regency**
- **1954 – 'Stardust', based on a Daimler DK400**
- **1955 – 'Golden Zebra', based on a Daimler DK400** *Illustrated below*

In 2006 auctioneer Bonhams sold the 'Golden Zebra', now fully restored, for £177,500, almost doubling its estimate.

* A mysterious sixth 'Docker Daimler' would have been a Daimler 104-based coupé with a lightweight aluminium body. It made an appearance at the 1956 London Motor Show with none of the usual fanfare.

The longest traffic jams ever

Think your commute to work is a slog? These are the longest traffic jams ever (for which reliable data is available):

Length	Date	Place
410 miles (656 km)	4 August 2001	Paris–Toulouse, France
109 miles (174 km)	16 February 1980	Lyon, France
90 miles (144 km)	21 December 2001	Bavaria, Germany
84 miles (134 km)	12 August 1990	Tokyo, Japan
70 miles (112 km)	24 August 2001	Staffordshire/Cheshire, UK

The biggest pre-1939 traffic jam is thought to have occurred on 21 May 1927 at Le Bourget, Paris, when 12,000 cars queued to see aviator Charles Lindbergh arrive from his pioneering transatlantic flight.

When cars outnumbered drivers

The Bureau of Transportation Statistics in the United States found that in 2003, for the first time, the number of private vehicles on American roads was greater than the number of registered driving-licence holders. There were 204 million cars and trucks (pick-ups and sport utility vehicles) and 191 million drivers. That's an average of 1.9 privately owned vehicles and 1.8 drivers for every one of the 107 million households in the country.

The last time a similar survey had been conducted, in 1995, the two numbers had been almost identical. 'We've added more cars than people for the last two decades, and the average number of people per household has been declining', said Alan Pisarski, author of *Commuting in America*. 'This is the final realization of the American ethos', added the director of Virginia Tech's Metropolitan Institute, a regional-growth think-tank. 'There's a real love of the road.'

The 15 fastest production cars of all time

Some Porsches, Chevrolet Corvettes and other cars have been modified by specialists to go faster, but these are the original models, on general sale to the public at a list price, that will reach a higher top speed than any others:

Bugatti Veyron 16.4	253 mph (405 km/h)
Koenigsegg CCX	250 mph (400 km/h)
SSC Aero	249 mph (398 km/h)
Saleen S7 *Illustrated below*	248 mph (397 km/h)
Koenigsegg CCR	241 mph (386 km/h)
Koenigsegg 8S	240 mph (384 km/h)
McLaren F1	240 mph (384 km/h)
Bristol Fighter T	225 mph (360 km/h)
Ferrari Enzo	220 mph (352 km/h)
Pagani Zonda C12 F	214 mph (342 km/h)
Jaguar XJ220	213 mph (341 km/h)
Bugatti EB110	212 mph (339 km/h)
Lamborghini Murcielago LP640	211 mph (338 km/h)
Mercedes SLR 722 Edition	209 mph (334 km/h)
Porsche Carrera GT	207 mph (333 km/h)

The Porsche family tree: how the Porsches and Piëchs are related

In early 2007 came the surprise announcement that car-industry minnow Porsche had built up a 30.9 per cent stake in the giant Volkswagen. Former star Audi engineer and Volkswagen chairman Ferdinand Piëch also happens to own about 13 per cent of Porsche. He is related to Volkswagen Beetle designer and Porsche founder Ferdinand Porsche. This family tree shows how:

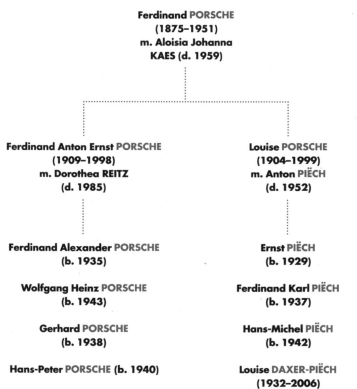

Ferdinand PORSCHE
(1875–1951)
m. Aloisia Johanna
KAES (d. 1959)

Ferdinand Anton Ernst PORSCHE
(1909–1998)
m. Dorothea REITZ
(d. 1985)

Louise PORSCHE
(1904–1999)
m. Anton PIËCH
(d. 1952)

Ferdinand Alexander PORSCHE
(b. 1935)

Ernst PIËCH
(b. 1929)

Wolfgang Heinz PORSCHE
(b. 1943)

Ferdinand Karl PIËCH
(b. 1937)

Gerhard PORSCHE
(b. 1938)

Hans-Michel PIËCH
(b. 1942)

Hans-Peter PORSCHE (b. 1940)

Louise DAXER-PIËCH
(1932–2006)

How to wash your car

If you value your car's bodywork, you'll want to make sure it is washed properly. These 10 steps, compiled with help from leading car-care products company Autoglym, will give a sparkling result:

1 Before you start, make sure the aerial is down, so you don't poke yourself in the eye, and that the wipers are parked halfway up the windscreen. Avoid washing the car in hot, direct sunlight.

2 Give your car a thorough blast of water, using the highest setting on a high-pressure hose, especially around sills, bumpers and wheel arches, to loosen off mud and grit. Start at the sills and work upwards, but don't drag the hose over the car because it might scratch paintwork.

3 Altering the setting, rain a fine spray of water all over the car to wet it thoroughly.

4 Using a good car shampoo (never, ever, washing-up liquid, which contains corrosive salts) mixed with tepid water, sponge over one side of the car, working downwards from the roof. Wide sweeps with plenty of water will ease off the grime.

5 After gently hosing down, repeat on the other side. Use a small, soft brush to push the shampoo into crevices around the bumpers, grille, lights and badges; flush it out again before it dries.

6 Never let the bodywork dry out before you rinse off the shampoo, or the finished car will look streaky.

7 Shift engrained brake dust on wheels with a specialist wheel cleaner, and use a proper glass cleaner on windows. A car wash is also the best time to check that the screenwashers are functioning, replenish their water supply and check for split windscreen-wiper blades.

8 Surplus surface water can be chased off using a flexible rubber blade, which should be cleaned off after each sweep to avoid scratching the paintwork.

9 A chamois leather, preferably a synthetic version, should then be used to soak up the rest of the water. In really wet areas, use it laid out flat to get the most off, and then wipe dry as normal. Use the edge of the leather to soak up water around bumpers and other nooks and crannies.

10 Also use the leather around the edges of all the doors and the boot, and then open and slam the doors and boot a couple of times to dislodge trapped water; leave the doors open for a while afterwards so it all drains away.

The origins of Indian cars

With high import duties and a government keen to encourage its own car industry, India was for years a motoring backwater where obsolete Western and Japanese models gained a new lease of life under unfamiliar names. Today the market is opening up to foreign manufacturers, and the cars on India's roads are beginning to look identical to the Chevrolets, Fiats, Fords and Toyotas found elsewhere. But here are 15 exclusively Indian models from the recent past and the cars on which they are based:

Hindustan 10	Morris 10
Hindustan Ambassador	Morris Oxford II
Hindustan Baby	Morris Minor
Hindustan Contessa	Vauxhall Victor FE
Hindustan Landmaster	Morris Oxford MO series
Mahindra	Willys Jeep
Maruti 800	Suzuki Alto
Maruti Esteem	Suzuki Swift
Premier 118NE *Illustrated below*	Fiat 124
Premier Padmini	Fiat 1100
Sipani D1	Daihatsu Charade
Sipani Dolphin	Reliant Kitten
Sipani Montana	Reliant Kitten
Standard 2000	Rover SD1
Standard Gazel	Triumph Herald

The death toll from road traffic accidents

As more and more people around the world get behind the wheel, so the death toll on our roads is rising. It is estimated that in 1999 there were 800,000 fatalities caused by road traffic accidents (RTAs). This figure is forecast to rise to 1.2 million by 2010, and will probably hit at least 1.3 million by 2020. In that time, analysts estimate that road traffic injuries will become a big health issue – leaping from ninth to third in the list of the leading contributors to the global burden of disease or injury.

This is a list of RTA fatalities in each country per one billion vehicle kilometres travelled, as at 2003. It shows that the roads are over six times more dangerous in Slovakia than in Finland ... and that you are safest on the roads of highly developed economies or those in vast, under-populated areas.

Country	Deaths*	Country	Deaths*
SLOVAKIA	46.9	ITALY	10.9
CZECH REPUBLIC	31.7	DENMARK	9.7
GREECE	26.7	GERMANY	9.7
SOUTH KOREA	26	USA	9.4
SLOVENIA	16.7	CANADA	8.9
BELGIUM	16.3	SWITZERLAND	8.8
ICELAND	16	NORWAY	8.3
NEW ZEALAND	12.4	SWEDEN	8.3
AUSTRIA	11.7	AUSTRALIA	8
JAPAN	11.2	THE NETHERLANDS	7.7
FRANCE	10.9	FINLAND	7.6
IRELAND	10.9	UK	7.6

* (per billion vehicle km travelled)

The minimum age limits for driving a car

There seems to be a growing international consensus that 18 is the appropriate minimum age at which to start driving. The exceptions are mainly in remote territories where public transport is not an alternative. This list shows the minimum age for rookie drivers around the world:

ALBANIA	18	MALTA	18
AUSTRALIA	18	MAURITIUS	18
AUSTRIA	17	THE NETHERLANDS	18
BELGIUM	18	NEW ZEALAND	15
BRAZIL	18	NORWAY	18
CANADA	16*	OMAN	18
CHINA	18	PAKISTAN	18
CYPRUS	18	POLAND	17
DENMARK	18	PORTUGAL	18
ETHIOPIA	14	RUSSIA	18
FINLAND	18	SOUTH AFRICA	18
FRANCE	18	SPAIN	18
GERMANY	18	SWEDEN	18
ICELAND	17	SWITZERLAND	18
INDIA	18	TAIWAN	18
IRELAND	17	TANZANIA	18
ITALY	18	UK	17
JAPAN	18	URUGUAY	18
LUXEMBOURG	18	USA	14–17**
MALAYSIA	17	VENEZUELA	18

* 17 in Saskatchewan and Newfoundland; 18 in New Brunswick   ** depending on state

Animals on car badges

Along with coats of arms, national flags and speed-suggestive wings, animals are among the most commonly featured motifs on car emblems. These are the marques and the creatures that are mostly associated with them through their appearance on bonnets:

Marque	Country	Animal
Abarth	ITALY	scorpion
Alfa Romeo	ITALY	snake
Argyll	UK	lion

Marque	Country	Animal
Bean	UK	lion
Bianchi	ITALY	eagle
Chenard-Walcker	FRANCE	eagle
DFP	UK	greyhound
Dodge	USA	ram *Illustrated below, left*
Duesenberg	USA	eagle
Ferrari	ITALY	horse
Gordon Keeble	UK	tortoise
Holden	AUSTRALIA	lion
Jaguar	UK	jaguar
Lamborghini	ITALY	bull
Morris	UK	ox
Perodua	MALAYSIA	deer
Peugeot	FRANCE	lion *Illustrated below, centre*
Porsche	GERMANY	horse *Illustrated below, right*
Proton	MALAYSIA	tiger
Shelby	USA	cobra
Simca	FRANCE	swallow
Stanley	USA	horses
Sunbeam-Talbot	UK	dog
Swift	UK	swift
Voisin	FRANCE	scarab beetle
Volga	RUSSIA	stag
Volkswagen (early)	GERMANY	wolf

Mythical creatures have also appeared on car badges, including merlettes on the Cadillac badge, Pegasus on the Pegaso badge, griffins on Kiefts, Saabs, Turners and Vauxhalls, a dragon on Gilberns, a sea-unicorn on Lea-Francis cars and a sphinx on Armstrong Siddeleys.

A guide to world rallying terms

The World Rally Championship (WRC) was established in 1973. Unlike in Formula One, rally racing uses 'real' cars competing against one another in timed events over a course through varied terrain. Rally cars are based on production models, which they must resemble, but are vastly more powerful and are custom-built to withstand tough treatment. They have built-in radio communication systems so the driver and co-driver can talk to each other and also to the team's base. Rally cars cost up to £350,000 apiece.

There are three main WRC classes:

World Rally Cars

A relatively new classification, these generally feature four-wheel drive, a turbocharged 2-litre engine and highly developed suspension, cooling and electronics.

Group N

Cars in this class usually feature four-wheel drive and a turbocharged 2-litre engine but fewer other modifications.

Junior WRC

Cars in this class mostly have front-wheel drive, a 1.6-litre normally aspirated (non-turbocharged) engine and few modifications.

The cars can compete for both class and overall positions. In addition to drivers and co-drivers, rally teams include up to 60 people: there are specialists in engineering and tyres, as well as caterers, co-ordinators, doctors, fitness instructors, managers, press officers and physiotherapists who travel the world to each event.

The WRC for 2007 (a typical year) included these rallies, taking place from January to December:

Rallye Automobile Monte Carlo	January
Swedish Rally	February
Rally Norway	February
Rally Mexico	March
Rallye de Portugal	March/April
Rally Argentina	May
Rally d'Italia Sardegna (Sardinia)	May
Acropolis Rally (Greece)	June
Rally Finland	August
Rallye Deutschland (Germany)	August
Rally New Zealand	August/September
Rally Catalunya (Spain)	October
Rallye de France	October
Rally Japan	October
Rally Ireland	November
Wales Rally (UK)	November/December

Since 2002 the WRC has run its points system in the same way as Formula One. The overall classification is as follows:

1st	**10 points**		5th	**4 points**
2nd	**8 points**		6th	**3 points**
3rd	**6 points**		7th	**2 points**
4th	**5 points**		8th	**1 point**

The WRC world is full of jargon that can be hard for the outsider to understand. Here are some of the most commonly encountered words and terms explained:

anti-lag	an engine-management system in which half the fuel is burned in the exhaust manifold instead of the engine; this keeps the turbocharger spinning during gear changes or braking.
co-driver	the 'navigator' who relays the course notes to the driver; does not actually drive the car.

Continued from previous page

crew	the driver and co-driver.
cutting	to cut corners to get around bends faster.
diffs	short for 'differentials' – front and rear devices that distribute power to front and back wheels on four-wheel-drive cars.
gravel crew	the team members responsible for updating notes with data on weather conditions two hours before the rally begins.
hairpin	a slow, 180-degree turn, often taken with the help of the handbrake.
ISC	stands for International Sportsworld Communicators, the owner of WRC commercial and TV rights.
leg	a part of a rally, usually a day.
notes	detailed descriptions of an event's topography, usually individually compiled by each driver/co-driver partnership on a slow-speed reconnaissance ('recce') run before the actual rally.
pace notes	anticipated speeds, recorded in the notes, at various points on a rally.
parc exposé	a display of all the cars in an event for public enjoyment.
parc fermé	all competing rally cars parked together and cordoned off (often overnight).
regrouping	a scheduled stop when all the remaining cars on a rally come together before tackling the worst leg, but not for servicing.
road section	part of a rally route (not always part of the competitive element) on public roads where cars must obey local traffic laws.
scrutineering	pre- and post-rally inspection of cars, equipment and even clothing by organizers to ensure they meet all regulations.
service	when team technicians work on the car, generally in a service area where all the teams are encamped; only the driver and co-driver can work on the car in the timed event.
special stage	a timed competitive section of road or terrain closed to public traffic. Most rallies include more than 20 such stages. A super-special stage is held in a designated area or course, often with spectator facilities.
tarmac	asphalt roads used in rallies.
time allowed	the period from when the car leaves the start to when it crosses the finishing line. Penalties are incurred if this is not followed.
time control	marshals who time the event.
turbo lag	a slight delay in power delivery caused by the split-second difference in speed between the turbocharger and engine revs.

The world's top car-producing nations

These are the nations that make the most cars and light trucks, according to the latest official figures supplied by each country's automotive industry trade body:

Country	Number of cars produced (2005)	Country	Number of cars produced (2005)
USA	11,524,000	BRAZIL	2,375,000
JAPAN	10,064,000	UK	1,783,000
GERMANY	5,543,000	MEXICO	1,607,000
CHINA	5,067,000	INDIA	1,406,000
SOUTH KOREA	3,657,000	RUSSIA	1,264,000
FRANCE	3,495,000	THAILAND	1,110,000
SPAIN	2,677,000	ITALY	996,000
CANADA	2,624,000		

Ferrari's strict colour code

Italian sports-car legend Ferrari sold 5671 road cars in 2006 and claims that every single one was unique in the way it had been personalized for its lucky owner. Ferrari has, however, lain down specific ground rules when it comes to paintwork. The Maranello factory offers a standard range of 16 colours from which to choose. At extra charge, Ferrari will provide paintwork in any colour that has been used on a previous model, although it sets a limit of a single yellow and three shades of red:

Rosso Corsa	traditional Ferrari red
Rosso Monza	metallic red
Rosso Scuderia	Formula One red (slightly orange)

However, for its 612 Scaglietti, Ferrari launched an exclusive palette of 10 'historic' paint options, all of which have been used on classic models in the past, so that serious collectors can co-ordinate their new cars with their old ones. The colours are:

Avio	bright blue
Avorio	ivory
Azzurro	medium blue
Blu Scozia	dark navy blue
Celeste	aquamarine
Grigio Ferro	metallic iron-grey
Grigio Medio	pastel mid-grey
Grigio Scuro	pastel anthracite
Verde Abetone	pastel green
Vinaccia	dark cherry

The Peugeot pepper mill

You need to thank Peugeot for the consistency of your seasoning whenever you eat out. Peugeot pepper mills are the number-one choice of chefs and restaurants. And, but for the brilliance of their mechanisms, Peugeot cars wouldn't exist.

Peugeot was already big in quality ironmongery when, in 1842, it invented the pepper mill. Its patented design combined two, previously manual, functions, cracking the peppercorns before grinding the pieces finely and evenly. The secret lay in the case-hardened steel Peugeot used, and the mechanism was so reliable that it's remained unchanged ever since. 'The grind is very even,' said Richard Gilbert of regional distributor Gilberts Food Equipment, 'so chefs like them for recipes – you don't get any nasty chunks of pepper, or any flakes. All other mill mechanisms are moulded or cast – Peugeots are so good because they're individually machine-cut.'

Peugeot soon expanded into salt mills, coffee grinders, umbrella frames and bicycle-wheel spokes. It then became France's leading bike manufacturer and in 1889 diversified into another newfangled area: the motor car.

Peugeot pepper mills are available in various sizes, ranging from 4.5 inches (11.5 cm) to 48 inches (120 cm), in plain beech wood – the classic, which has been available for more than 160 years – and stainless-steel or acrylic-bodied versions. And all Peugeot mills and mechanisms come with something unheard of in the car world – an unlimited lifetime guarantee.

The forgotten ancestors of today's MPVs

The first multi-purpose vehicle (MPV) as the world knows it today made its debut in 1983. It was the Chrysler 'Minivan', which was marketed initially as the Dodge Caravan or near-identical Plymouth Voyager. A commercial van version was later made, but this car was designed primarily as a roomy and tall passenger vehicle, the interior of which could be altered in several different ways for various passenger/cargo configurations. A year later, Renault took the wraps off its eight-seater Espace, which added styling and driving verve to the Chrysler concept. Together, the two cars started a brand-new trend in the car market. Yet, novel as the Minivan and Espace were, they were by no means the first vehicles to attempt to crack the 'people-first' design idea. Now largely forgotten, these nine automotive projects, which started more than 70 years ago, got there first:

- **Stout Scarab 1935** Aircraft designer William B. Stout envisaged this as a mobile office, and the cockpit was separate from the passenger area, as in a plane's fuselage. Just nine were sold (of which five still exist), including one to chewing-gum king Philip K. Wrigley.

- **Renault Juvaquatre Taxi 1945** The winner of a design competition in Paris, this 'one-box' design by Escoffier and engineer Jacques Rousseau had sliding doors and other MPV features.

- **Volkswagen Kombi 1950** Really a Type 2 Transporter van with side windows and removable passenger seats in the back – but the first of its kind. The name is the shortening of the German *Kombinationskraftwagen* (combination vehicle), indicating its versatility.

- **Fiat 600 Multipla 1956** With three rows of two seats and based on the rear-engined Fiat 600 economy car, this bonnet-less version was extremely compact in the 'one-box' manner. The driver sat above the front wheels in the tiny six-seater, which was popular as a taxi in Italy. *Illustrated opposite.*

- **Mercury Palomar 1962** A concept design from Ford with three rows of two seats ... despite having only two doors. The modular interior had a swivelling front passenger seat, and the rearmost bench seat could face either way.

- **Daihatsu BCX-III 1973** A forgotten show car never marketed to the public, this low-slung six-seater estate gave access to the rear four seats via rear doors that popped out and slid forward.

- **Toyota MP-1 1975** Had this Toyota Crown-based prototype been put into production, it would have been an MPV exactly as we knowsuch vehicles today: tall passenger area, sliding doors, bonnet falling away to give a slanted nose – it even had wheelchair access.

- **Nissan Prairie 1982** This boxy Japanese estate, with the emphasis firmly on family practicality, drew on designs by Italy's Giorgetto Giugiaro (such as the 1978 Lancia Megagamma) for raised height and commanding driving position. Still only a five-seater.

- **Toyota Space Cruiser Model F 1983** This was almost the world's first MPV – but not quite, as it was actually a rebodied Toyota Liteace van. It could seat eight in luxurious car-like comfort, but had the top-heavy driving characteristics of the commercial vehicle beneath.

A wretched round-up of roadkill

Wildlife, and indeed domestic pets, pay a terrible price for our motoring freedom. *Animal People* magazine estimates that mammals are mown down annually on American roads in the following numbers:

Squirrels	41,000,000	**Raccoons**	15,000,000
Cats	26,000,000	**Dogs**	6,000,000
Rats	22,000,000	**Deer**	350,000
Opossums	19,000,000		

The Mammals Trust UK, among other sources, provides the following data for massacred mammals on the other side of the Atlantic:

Rabbits	800,000	**Deer**	50,000
Foxes	100,000	**Squirrels**	50,000
Badgers	50,000	**Hedgehogs**	15,000

Japan's unique 'K'-car rules

Japan has a unique set of taxation rules that has led to the growth of the small cars and vans so peculiar to the country – the Kei- or 'K'-class. The impetus for these has been to persuade drivers to opt for tiny vehicles, in both overall size and in engine capacity. 'K' cars attract lower tax and insurance rates, but, most im- portantly, their owners do not have to prove that they have a dedicated parking space in which to keep their car – as other motorists are obliged to do in the crowded nation. The rules originated after World War II, at a time when many Japanese people were considering trading in their motorcycles for cars, and when businesses were modernizing their delivery systems.

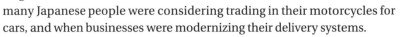

'K' cars are today known in English-speaking circles as 'yellow-plate cars' on account of their black-on-yellow (private cars) and yellow-on-black (commercial vehicles) number plates. They often come loaded with equipment and gadgets that belie their tiny size: turbochargers, automatic transmission and four-wheel drive are common.

Nissan and Toyota are conspicuous by their absence in the 'K'-car arena. The manufacturers that offer 'K' cars are Daihatsu, Honda, Mazda, Mitsubishi, Subaru and Suzuki. Smart is the only non-Japanese company to offer a car, the Fortwo, matching the 'K'-car class criteria. This is how the 'K'-car class rules have changed over the years:

Date	Max. length	Max. width	Max. height	Max. engine size	Max. power
8.7.1949	2.8 m (9 ft 2 in.)	1 m (3 ft 3 in.)	2 m (6 ft 7 in.)	150 cc†	any
26.7.1950	3 m (9 ft 10 in.)	1.3 m (4 ft 3 in.)	2 m (6 ft 7 in.)	300 cc††	any
16.8.1951	3 m (9 ft 10 in.)	1.3 m (4 ft 3 in.)	2 m (6 ft 7 in.)	360 cc†††	any
4.4.1955	3 m (9 ft 10 in.)	1.3m (4 ft 3 in.)	2 m (6 ft 7 in.)	360 cc	any
1.1.1976	3.2 m (10 ft 6 in.)	1.4 m (4 ft 7 in.)	2 m (6 ft 7 in.)	550 cc	any
1.3.1990	3.3 m (10 ft 9 in.)	1.4 m (4 ft 7 in.)	2 m (6 ft 7 in.)	660 cc	64 bhp
1.10.1998	3.4m (11 ft 1 in.)	1.48 m (4 ft 10 in.)	2 m (6 ft 7 in.)	660 cc	64 bhp

† for a four-stroke engine – 100 cc for a two-stroke
†† for a four-stroke engine – 200 cc for a two-stroke
††† for a four-stroke engine – 240 cc for a two-stroke

Cars with concealed headlights

The idea of hiding the headlights on a car first occurred to the designer Gordon Buehrig in 1936 when he created the Cord 810, the first car with headlights that retracted into the vehicle's mudguards; they were actually modified Stinson aircraft landing lights (the Cord was also the first car to have its body shape registered as an original design). Since then, dozens of others have copied the idea, using a variety of ways to conceal the headlights for both aesthetic and aerodynamic reasons – the lower a car's nose, the more effectively it cuts through the air. However, the last car launched with concealed headlamps was the Ferrari 456 GT in 1992. Tighter design legislation relating to frontal impact effects on pedestrians means that, even though they have not been banned by legislators, the old 'flip-up' headlights synonymous with the supercars of the 1970s have become a thing of the past.

This is a list of all the production cars there have been with concealed headlights, plus the method of concealment used in each case:

AC ME3000 (1973)
flip-up

Alpine A610 (1991)
flip-up

Aston Martin Lagonda (1976)
flip-up

Bitter CD (1974)
flip-up

Bitter SC (1979)
flip-up

BMW 8 Series (1990)
flip-up *Illustrated above*

BMW M1 (1979)
flip-up

Bricklin SV-1 (1974)
flip-up

Buick Reatta (1986)
flip-up

Buick Riviera (1965)
'clamshell'-covered

Cadillac Eldorado (1967)
rotating retractable

Chevrolet Camaro (1967)
sliding light covers

Chevrolet Caprice (1969)
rotating retractable (optional)

Chevrolet Corvette (1983)
flip-up

Chevrolet Corvette Sting Ray (1963)
rotating retractable

Chevrolet Corvette Stingray (1968)
flip-up

Chrysler 300 (1968)
rotating retractable

Chrysler Imperial (1981)
retractable light covers

Chrysler LeBaron (1987)
retractable light covers

Chrysler New Yorker (1976)
retractable light covers

Chrysler New Yorker (1988)
retractable light covers

Cizeta V16T (1989)
flip-up

Continued from previous page

Clan II (1984)
flip-up

Cord 812 (1936)
retractable

Davrian (1968)
flip-up

De Soto (1942)
retractable

De Tomaso Guara (1993)
flip-up

De Tomaso Pantera (1969)
flip-up

Dodge Charger (1966)
rotating retractable

Dodge Daytona (1987)
flip-up

Dodge Monaco (1972)
retractable light covers

Eagle Talon (1990)
flip-up

Ferrari 288 GTO (1984)
flip-up

Ferrari 348 (1989)
flip-up

Ferrari 365 GT4/400 GT/412 (1972)
flip-up

Ferrari 365 GTB/4 Daytona (1968)
flip-up

Ferrari 365 GTC/365 GTC4 (1968)
flip-up

Ferrari 456 GT (1992)
flip-up

Ferrari 512 BB (1973)
flip-up

Ferrari Dino 208/308 GT4 (1973)
flip-up

Ferrari Dino 208/308 GTB/S and 328 GTB/S (1975)
flip-up

Ferrari F355 (1994)
flip-up

Ferrari Mondial (1980)
flip-up

Ferrari Testarossa (1984)
flip-up

Fiat X1/9 (1972)
flip-up

Ford/Mercury Capri (1991)
flip-up

Ford Galaxie 500 XL (1968)
retractable light covers

Ford LTD (1970)
sliding light covers

Ford LTD (1975)
retractable light covers

Ford Probe (1989)
flip-up

Ford Thunderbird (1967)
retractable light covers

Ford Thunderbird (1977)
retractable light covers

Ford Torino Brougham (1970)
retractable light covers

Honda Accord/Accord Aerodeck (1985)
flip-up

Honda Integra (1986)
flip-up

Honda NSX (1990)
flip-up

Honda Prelude (1983)
flip-up

Imperial (1969)
retractable headlight covers

Iso Lele (1969)
part-concealed under lifting covers

Isuzu Impulse/Piazza (1981)
part-covered

Jaguar XJ220 (1992)
rotating retractable

Lamborghini Countach (1974)
flip-up

Lamborghini Diablo (1990)
flip-up

Lamborghini Islero (1968)
flip-up

Lamborghini Jarama (1970)
flip-up

Lamborghini Uracco/Silhouette/Jalpa (1970)
flip-up

Lancia Stratos (1973)
flip-up

Lincoln Continental III/IV (1968)
retractable light covers

Lincoln Mark series (1968)
retractable light covers

Lotus Eclat/Excel (1975)
flip-up

Lotus Elan (1962)
rotating retractable

Lotus Elan (1989)
flip-up

Lotus Elan + 2 (1969)
rotating retractable

Lotus Elite (1974)
flip-up

Lotus Esprit (1976)
flip-up

Maserati Bora (1971)
flip-up
Maserati Ghibli (1967)
flip-up
Maserati Indy (1969)
flip-up
Maserati Khamsin (1973)
flip-up
Maserati Merak (1972)
flip-up
Matra Bagheera (1973)
flip-up
Matra M530 (1968)
flip-up
Matra Murena (1980)
flip-up
Mazda 323F (1989)
flip-up
Mazda 929 (1981)
flip-up
Mazda MX-5 (1989)
flip-up
Mazda RX-7 (1978)
flip-up
Mazda RX-7 (1986)
flip-up
Mercury Cougar (1967)
rotating retractable
Mercury Marquis (1969)
rotating retractable
Mercury Montego (1970)
rotating retractable
Mitsubishi 3000GT (1991)
flip-up
Mitsubishi Eclipse (1990)
flip-up

Mitsubishi Starion (1982)
flip-up
Nissan 200 SX (1989)
flip-up
Nissan 300 ZX (1984)
flip-up
Nissan Silvia ZX (1984)
flip-up
Oldsmobile Toronado (1966)
rotating retractable
Oldsmobile Toronado (1986)
drop-down covers
Opel GT (1968)
rotating retractable
Panther Solo (1989)
revolving retractable
Plymouth Fury (1970)
retractable light covers
Plymouth Laser (1991)
flip-up
Pontiac Fiero (1984)
flip-up
Pontiac Firebird (1982)
flip-up
Pontiac Grand Prix (1967)
rotating light covers
Pontiac GTO (1968)
rotating light covers
Porsche 911 Turbo SE (1985)
flip-up
Porsche 924 (1976)
flip-up
Porsche 928 (1977)
lie-flat
Porsche 944 (1982)
flip-up
Porsche 968 (1991)
lie-flat
Rapport Ritz (1981)
concealed under lifting aerofoil

Reliant Scimitar Sabre (1993)
flip-up
Reliant Scimitar SS1 (1984)
lie-flat
Saab Sonett III (1970)
flip-up
Saturn SC2 (1991)
flip-up
Subaru XT (1985)
flip-up
Toyota 2000 GT (1967)
flip-up
Toyota Celica (1983)
flip-up
Toyota Celica (1985)
flip-up
Toyota Celica (1986)
flip-up
Toyota Celica (1989)
flip-up
Toyota Celica Supra (1982)
flip-up
Toyota Corolla GT-S/ SR5 Sprinter Trueno (1983)
flip-up
Toyota MR2 (1984)
flip-up
Triumph TR7 (1975)
flip-up
TVR Tasmin/280/350/ 390/420 (1980)
flip-up
Venturi (1985)
flip-up
Vignale-Fiat 125 Samantha (1967)
lie-flat
Volkswagen-Porsche 914/916 (1969)
flip-up
Volvo 480 ES (1987)
flip-up

10 archaic phrases for drivers, in six languages

Times change; unless you're driving an unreliable classic car, or you're in the most remote of locales, chances are you won't ever need to say these phrases again when travelling far from home. However, just in case, here they are:

1 ENGLISH **Please fill the tank with Premium Grade.**
FRENCH — Voulez-vous faire le plein avec Super.
DUTCH — Wilt u de tank vullen met Super.
GERMAN — Geben Sie mir bitte Super.
ITALIAN — Faccia il pieno con Supercarburante.
SPANISH — Por favor llene el tanque con Super 90 octanos.

2 ENGLISH **Please check the oil level in the gearbox and back axle.**
FRENCH — Voulez-vous vérifier le niveau d'huile de la boite et du pont.
DUTCH — Wilt u de oile van der versnellingsbak en de achterbrug controleren.
GERMAN — Prüfen Sie bitte den Ölstand im Getriebe and in der Hinterachse.
ITALIAN — Controlli il livello dell'olio nel cambio e nel differenziale.
SPANISH — Por favor verifique el nivel de aceite de la caja de cambios y el diferencial.

3 ENGLISH **Would you help me get my car out of the ditch?**
FRENCH — Pouvez-vous m'aider à sortir ma voiture du fossé?
DUTCH — Wilt u mij helpen mijn wagen uit de sloot te halen?
GERMAN — Würden Sie mir helfen, den Wagen aus dem Graben zu ziehen?
ITALIAN — Potete aiutarmi a tirare la macchina fuori dal fosso?
SPANISH — ¿Me ayudaria Usted a sacar mi coche de la cuneta?

4 ENGLISH **I have had a puncture; will you please repair it?**
FRENCH — L'un de mes pneus est crevé. Voulez-vous le réparer?
DUTCH — Ik heb een lekke band; wilt u deze reparen?
GERMAN — Ich habe ein Reifenpanne gehabt. Reparieren Sie bitte den Reifen.
ITALIAN — Ho avuto una foratura, favourite repararla.
SPANISH — ¿He tenido un pinchazo y le ruego lo repare?

5 ENGLISH **Will you please grease my car?**
FRENCH — Veuillez faire un graissage complet de ma voiture.
DUTCH — Wilt u mijn wagen doorsmeren.
GERMAN — Bitte schmieren Sie den Wagen ab.
ITALIAN — Favorite ingrassare la mia vettura.
SPANISH — Por favor engrase mi coche.

6 ENGLISH **The carburettor needs adjusting.**
FRENCH — Le carburateur a besoin d'un réglage.
DUTCH — De carburateur moet bijgesteld worden.
GERMAN — Der Vergaser muß neu eingestellt werden.
ITALIAN — Occorre regolare il carburatore.
SPANISH — El carburador necesita ajuste.

7 ENGLISH   **The clutch needs re-lining.**
FRENCH   Il faut changer la garniture d'embrayage.
DUTCH   De koppeling moet opnieuw bekleed worden.
GERMAN   Der Kupplungsbelag muß erneuert werden.
ITALIAN   La frizione ha bisogno di una nuova guarnizione.
SPANISH   El embrague necesita discos neuvos.

8 ENGLISH   **The front wheels need adjusting.**
FRENCH   It faut régler le train avant.
DUTCH   De voorwielen moeten bijgesteld worden.
GERMAN   Die Spur der Vorderrader muß nachgestellt werden.
ITALIAN   Le ruote anteriori hanno bisogno di essere registrate.
SPANISH   Las ruedas delanteras necesitan ajuste.

9 ENGLISH   **There is something wrong with the dynamo.**
FRENCH   Il y a quelque chose qui ne va pas dans la dynamo.
DUTCH   Er is iets niet in orde met de dynamo.
GERMAN   Es ist etwas nicht in Ordnung an der Lichtmaschine.
ITALIAN   Vi e qualcosa che non va nella dinamo.
SPANISH   Hay alguna averia en la dinamo.

10 ENGLISH   **The engine needs decarbonizing.**
FRENCH   Le moteur a besoin d'un décalaminage.
DUTCH   De motor moet ontkoold worden.
GERMAN   Die Rückstände im Motor müssen entfernt werden.
ITALIAN   Occorre togliere le incrostazioni al motore.
SPANISH   Hace falta descarbonizar el motor.

How air conditioning affects petrol consumption

Some carmakers recommend that you keep your car's air-conditioning system switched on all the time, no matter what the outside temperature; they claim that keeping all the components lubricated by continuously circulating the coolant fluid maintains the system at optimum condition. Car air-conditioning systems need a compressor to power them, however, and that takes its power source direct from the engine. This means that the engine has to work harder than it would normally, which makes it less efficient and so blunts both performance and fuel economy. It could mean it uses up to 10 per cent more fuel. The 'economy' setting on the climate-control system in many cars is the most fuel-efficient mode since this usually switches off the air conditioner's compressor.

Can speed humps damage your car?

Many residents welcome speed humps as a traffic-calming measure in their area, but drivers also worry that they could damage the suspension systems on their cars. Can this really happen? According to MIRA, the design and development company formerly known as the Motor Industry Research Association, the answer is yes – although no law-abiding driver will ever suffer. MIRA says that any repeated cycle will result, eventually, in a failure of such components as bushes, suspension arms and dampers, depending on the speed and angle of the repeated impacts. By hitting a hump too fast, or during high-speed braking and with suspension compressed, sudden damage could occur (a thousand large impacts or a million small ones can have the same effect).

Today, however, car suspension components are designed to last for life, and generally it's another failure that consigns a car to scrap. Highways agencies build humps to prescribed standards so that, at correct, steady speeds, their impact is well within the capability of any car.

20 fictional vehicles

These cars and trucks never existed beyond the cartoonist's drawing board, the computer screen, the film studio special-effects department or the written word on the page:

Name of vehicle	Source
6000 SUX car	**RoboCop** film
Batmobile car	**Batman** comic strip
Beermobile car	**The Simpsons** cartoon
The Betsy car	**The Betsy** novel
Boomerang Rapido car	**Flåklypa Grand Prix; Pinchcliffe Grand Prix (in UK/USA)** feature-length animation
Canyonero SUV	**The Simpsons** cartoon
Catillac car	**The Catillac Cats** cartoon
Christine car	**Christine** novel and film
Coruscant air taxi	**Star Wars** films
Hirondel car	**The Saint** novels and TV series
The Homer car	**The Simpsons** cartoon
Invisible Boatmobile car	**SpongeBob SquarePants** cartoon
Lexus Mag-lev car *Illustrated right*	**Minority Report** short story and film
Maibatsu Monstrosity SUV	**Grand Theft Auto III** computer game
Melmoth car	**Lolita** novel and film
Nike One 2022 car	**Gran Turismo 4** computer game
S.L.O.W.* car	**The Cat in the Hat** film
Speed Buggy car	**Speed Buggy** cartoon
Thundercougarfalconbird car	**Futurama** cartoon
Vaillante car	**Michel Vaillant** comic strip

*stands for Super Luxurious Omnidirectional Whatchamajigger

Countries where women are not allowed to drive

This is a complete list of nations around the world where women are banned by law from driving cars on public roads:

• SAUDI ARABIA*

*In this country, women are also not allowed to take taxis alone or to ride bicycles in public.

The world's most important coachbuilders

Until the advent of widespread 'unitary' monocoque car construction after 1945, virtually all cars came with a separate chassis and bodywork that was either the standard factory offering or else it could be custom-made to the owner's own choice. To provide this bodymaking service, the car industry included hundreds of individual coachbuilding companies. As the name implies, many had previously manufactured horse-drawn vehicles, but many more were specifically opened to cash in on the demand for individual car bodies – for which some customers were prepared to pay vast sums. The firms below are the most significant: some offered one-off craftsmanship, others near mass-production, and a few did both. As the motor industry rapidly adopted the integral chassis/body, the coachbuilding trade died, although a few names still remain as subcontractors, specialists, design bureaux or brand names:

Name	Country	Active	Typical product
Barker	UK	1900–54	limousine/sports saloon
Baur	GERMANY	1910 onwards	cabriolet
Bertone	ITALY	1921 onwards	GT coupé
Boneschi	ITALY	1921 onwards	luxury convertible
Brewster	USA	1905–38	luxury convertible
Castagna	ITALY	1906 onwards	luxury convertible
Chapron	FRANCE	1920–78	cabriolet
Derham	USA	1907–69	limousine
Dietrich	USA	1925–31	luxury convertible
Farina	ITALY	1919–53	luxury convertible
Figoni & Falaschi	FRANCE	1923–51	sporting convertible
Fleetwood	USA	1909–31	limousine
Freestone & Webb	UK	1923–56	sporting saloon
Frua	ITALY	1952–83	GT coupé
Ghia	ITALY	1915–2002	GT coupé
Graber	SWITZERLAND	1925–70	touring saloon
Gurney Nutting	UK	1919–54	convertible
H.J. Mulliner	UK	1900 onwards	saloon
Hooper	UK	1900 onwards	limousine

Illustrated opposite

James Young	**UK**	1908–67	sports saloon
Judkins	**USA**	1897–1941	convertible
Karmann	**GERMANY**	1902–today	cabriolet
Kellner	**FRANCE**	1903–38	sports saloon
Labourdette	**FRANCE**	1899–1949	sports cabriolet
Lebaron	**USA**	1920–41	limousine
Murphy	**USA**	1920–32	convertible
Park Ward	**UK**	1919–today	sports saloon
Pininfarina	**ITALY**	1930–today	sports car
Saoutchik	**FRANCE**	1906–55	sports convertible
Sodomka	**CZECHOSLOVAKIA**	1925–56	cabriolet
Touring	**ITALY**	1926–66	GT coupé
Vanden Plas	**BELGIUM/UK**	1902–2005	sports convertible
Vignale	**ITALY**	1945–75	sports car
Weymann	**FRANCE/UK/USA**	1921–32	saloon
Worblaufen	**SWITZERLAND**	1929–58	cabriolet
Zagato	**ITALY**	1919–today	GT coupé

Cars that have gone those extra miles

A precise list of the world's most-travelled cars is impossible to compile – some of the most extraordinary mileages are, no doubt, simply not known. Below, however, are some incredible examples of cars that just keep rolling on and on and on and on:

- One high-mileage fact that is under little doubt concerns the car that has survived the greatest driving distance of all. This is a 1976 Mercedes-Benz 240D that was bought new by taxi driver Gregorios Sachinidis of Thessaloniki, Greece. When the odometer reached 2.8 million miles (4.5 million km) – 82 circuits of the globe – in 2004, Sachinidis finally decided to pension off the car. It's now in the Mercedes-Benz Museum in Stuttgart, Germany.

- Another taxi driver, Joseph Vaillancourt from Montreal, Canada, notched up 1,403,848 miles (2,258,791 km) in his 1963 Plymouth Fury taxi, a black car with a red interior. During that time, however – unlike the Greek Mercedes – the vehicle got through five engines. The tally could have been higher still if the 73-year-old's pride-and-joy hadn't been smashed up by a truck in 2000. Happily, the car's new owner – Quebec actor Michel Barette – has spent $20,000 restoring it.
- Peter Gilbert, a British financial services salesman based in the United States in Glendale, Wisconsin, took his 1989 Saab 900 SPG to 1,001,385 miles (1,611,228 km) before finally donating it to the Wisconsin Automotive Museum in 2006. In less than two decades, it had consumed 600 quarts (568 litres) of synthetic Mobil-1 oil, two entire tanker-loads of petrol, 22 sets of tyres, three engine head gaskets and five transmissions.
- On account of the abuse they receive, vans tend to be worn out long before they reach large six-figure mileages. One honourable exception is a Mercedes-Benz Sprinter van belonging to Klaus Schade, a German newspaper courier. Between 1995 and 2005 it transported him 559,234 miles (8,999,998 km).
- In this high-mileage list, 339,600 miles (546,416 km) would appear to be the record of a motoring lightweight. But for a tiny Smart Fortwo city car still on its original three-cylinder engine, it's quite a feat. The car was owned by a German dental laboratory before being taken on by a motoring magazine.
- When Mercedes-Benz launched its 300SD in the United States in 1978, it began a nationwide 'Great Diesel Search' to find the most-travelled oil-burning example of the marque. Robert O'Reilly's 1957 Mercedes-Benz 180D came out top, the Olympia, Washington-based car having covered a genuine 1,184,800 miles (1,906,343 km). It was used extensively in the company's advertising campaigns during the 1980s.
- No review of high-mileage motoring is complete without mention of Irv Gordon and his 1966 Volvo P1800. In its fortieth year of ownership by Gordon, the car passed the 2,500,000-mile (4,022,500-km) mark, and the retired teacher from Long Island, New York, has now set his sights on a target of 3,000,000 miles (4,827,000 km); his annual mileage averages 100,000 miles (160,900 km), which alone is further than many other cars ever travel. How does he do it? Well …

Irv Gordon's 10 tips to make your car last a million miles

The king of the high-mileage car has this advice to give to anyone intending to keep and use their car for a long, long time:

1 Start with a car you like: 'To reach 2,000,000 miles [3,218,000 km], you're going to spend more than 40,000 hours driving if you average 50 mph [80 km/h]. This means your car is going to be a home away from home. If you don't like your car, you'll never go the distance.'

2 Change your oil and filter regularly: 'If there is any one maintenance activity that will extend the life of your car's engine, this is it. Considering the relatively low cost of oil and filters, this is the cheapest insurance policy your car will ever have.'

3 Use factory equipment parts: 'Avoid using parts by independent companies – go with factory parts. The people who built your car can afford to experiment more than you can in an effort to select the best part. Factory parts may sometimes be more expensive, but they are definitely compatible with your car.'

4 Use one brand of oil: 'Surprises are nice at birthday parties, but you don't want them under your car's hood. Using one brand of oil assures uniform quality and no surprises.'

5 Spend a few minutes a week checking under the bonnet: 'Even the most "mechanically challenged" car owners can look for low fluid levels or deterioration of belts and hoses. Also, look to see that the battery connections are tight and corrosion-free. These are the most common sources of trouble on the road.'

6 Wash your car regularly: 'Use a mild soap and wash your car by hand. In the winter, hose underneath the vehicle. A clean car gives you an excellent opportunity to look for small nicks and scratches, which may be touched up before rust begins to form.'

7 Wax the car twice a year: 'The value of waxing goes well beyond making your car look nicer than your neighbour's. It provides protection against oxidation and rust.'

8 Develop a good working relationship with your dealer and mechanic: 'Both are your partners over the long run. If they know you're a serious, regular customer, they'll give you the help and advice you need, as you need it.'

9 Use petrol from a high-volume station: 'Those old, country-store gas stations that look like relics are just that – relics. Without heavy traffic, the gasoline remains in their storage units for extended periods of time, which causes water contamination in their fuel supply because of condensation.'

10 When your car makes a funny noise, listen to it: 'Don't turn up the radio and hope that knocking noise goes away. If your car develops a condition, take it in and have it fixed quickly. The longer you wait, the greater potential for damage.'

The world's finest floating garage is no more

Until the luxury cruise liner *Queen Elizabeth 2* (*QE2*) was taken off its transatlantic route between Southampton and New York by cruise line Cunard, it had been possible to take a car with you on your journey. The iconic ship, launched in 1967, had a 12-car garage incorporated as an original feature. Indeed, in 1996, cars were ferried across the Atlantic as part of the centenary celebrations of the British motor industry.

Since 2003, however, the *QE2* has been undertaking cruises from Southampton to Norway and the Mediterranean, plus a single annual world cruise. The garage space has been turned over to stores to sustain the vessel's 1900 passengers on these voyages. In addition, new shipping rules effective from 1 January 2006 now outlaw cars on the *QE2* altogether.

The seven wonders of the road-bridge world

Talk of amazing bridges usually centres on the span of suspension bridges. Impressive engineering, for sure, but there are plenty of other astonishing structures that carry cars across otherwise insurmountable obstacles.

Bridge	Location	Measurement
World's tallest road viaduct	Millau Viaduct, France	270 m (886 ft) above ground
World's longest road viaduct	Millau Viaduct, France	2460 m (8070 ft)
World's longest suspension bridge	Akashi-Kaikyo, Japan	1991 m (6532 ft) – main span
World's longest causeway road	Lake Pontchartrain, Louisiana, USA	38.42 km (24³/₄ miles)
World's longest cable-stayed bridge	Sunshine Skyway Bridge, Florida, USA	8851 m (29,039 ft)
World's widest road bridge	Driscoll Bridge, New Jersey, USA	65.5 m (215 ft) – 21 lanes
World's longest floating bridge	Albert D. Rosellini Bridge, Washington, USA	2310 m (7580 ft)

Iran's thriving motor industry

Iran may be labouring under US-instigated trade sanctions, but even without the involvement of such American companies as General Motors, Ford and Chrysler, its Tehran-centred motor industry is a hive of activity. Japanese, Korean, European and Chinese manufacturers are happy to put politics aside and help local manufacturers provide a range of new and recent models for local consumers. Here's what's going on there:

Name	Town	Activity
Bonro	**Save**	assembly of SsangYong cars
Demik	**Tehran**	tuning of cars
Farassa	**Tehran**	manufacture of two-seater sports/racing cars
Fath	**Tehran**	manufacture of licence-built Toyota pick-ups
Hyundai	**Tehran**	assembly of Hyundai cars
Iran Khodro	**Tehran**	manufacture of Peugeot and own cars
Iran Rover	**Tehran**	manufacture of customized 4x4 vehicles
JMC	**Tehran**	manufacture of own-design 4x4 vehicles
Kish Khodro	**Tehran**	manufacture of own-design and Renault-based cars
Mazda	**Tehran**	assembly of Mazda cars and pick-ups
Mercedes-Benz	**Tehran**	assembly of Mercedes-Benz cars
Mitsubishi	**Tehran**	assembly of Mitsubishi Pajero
Morattab	**Tehran**	manufacture of version of Land Rover; assembly of SsangYongs
MVM	**Tehran**	assembly of Chery QQ cars
Pars Khodro	**Tehran**	assembly of Renaults and Nissans
Proton	**Tehran**	assembly of Proton Wira
Saipa	**Tehran**	assembly of Kias and Citroëns
Shabazzadeh	**Tehran**	manufacture of vintage-style convertible
Suzuki	**Tehran**	assembly of Vitara 4x4
Talash	**Tehran**	manufacture of three-wheeled city cars
Volkswagen	**Tehran**	assembly of Gol
Zamyad	**Tehran**	manufacture of Nissan pick-ups
Zarin	**Estahan**	manufacture of own-design Thunder 4x4

The secret history of the air ferry

In Britain in the 1940s there were no roll-on/roll-off ferries, much less a Channel Tunnel, to get drivers to mainland Europe: cars had to be craned on and off boats. But Air Commodore Griffith J. 'Taffy' Powell realized that the Bristol 170 Freighter aircraft, with giant 'clamshell' doors in its nose fronting its commodious freight bay, could easily take cars. Bristol lent him one, and on 7 July 1948, it took off from the grass airstrip at Lympne Airport, near Ashford in Kent, bound for Le Touquet in France. Powell and his own Armstrong Siddeley car were in-

side. The plane returned fully loaded with an extra car, and the world's only air ferry was up and running. Scheduled flights began the following week under the Silver City Airways banner.

Powell's new venture was a tremendous success. It transferred to Lydd Airport in 1954, which had a tarmac runway, and soon an uprated fleet of Bristol Superfreighters came into service, now able to swallow three cars and 20 passengers. It cost £25 per car and £4 for each passenger. The cars were driven up a ramp into the plane, while their owners settled down in the passenger compartment. The bumpy flight to Le Touquet took about 20 minutes, and the noisy propeller planes never rose above 3000 feet (915 m).

Silver City's service inspired one rival, the charmingly named Channel Air Bridge, flying between Southend and Calais, Ostend and Rotterdam. The company was at its peak in 1959. At high season, a plane would take off every 10 minutes, from 6 am until midnight. The Silver City spirit of adventure, however, was relatively short-lived. The introduction of new roll-on/roll-off ferries and hovercraft on cross-Channel routes in the 1960s killed off what had become British United Air Ferries. The last air car ferry took off from Lydd on 3 October 1970.

The contrasting lives of the car-rental kings

Their names are bywords for car hire the world over, but how much do we know about Messrs Hertz and Avis? Here's how their lives compared:

	Hertz	Avis
Name	John Daniel Hertz	Warren Edward Avis
Date of birth	10 April 1879	4 August 1915
Place of birth	Sklabina, Slovakia	Michigan, USA
First job in cars	Car salesman	Car trade investigator
Entered car hire	1923	1946
Route	Bought car-hire firm	Started own car-hire firm
First name	Hertz Drive-Ur-Self	Avis Airlines Rent-A-Car Systems
First cars for hire	Ford Model T	Ford (model unknown)
Car-hire achievement	Popularized car hire	Pioneered airport car hire
Personal achievement	General Motors board member	Sold out in 1954 for $8 million
Passion	Racehorses	Riding horses
Date of death	October 1961 (day unknown)	24 April 2007
Unlikely but true	Coined the term 'yellow cab'	Still waterskiing at 89

The meaning of the TIR sign

TIR stands for Transport International Routier, a customs system dating from 1975. The TIR is an internationally accepted customs document that covers journeys to and from and between European Union territory, North Africa and West Asian countries. To simplify border crossings, a vehicle or a container that has been satisfactorily examined by a customs officer – and awarded a TIR Carnet and sealed – will normally be free from further customs checks as it passes through other countries within the EU; the driver will not need to pay duties en route. The blue-and-white TIR sign is fixed to the front and rear of the vehicle or container and displayed to be clearly visible and within reach of the driver. The vetting of truck operators before they can participate in the scheme is very thorough.

The 10 most sought-after Scalextric cars

Scalextric, the slot-car racing system, was invented in 1957 by Fred Francis, a toy manufacturer who started out by making Scalex tinplate, clockwork model cars. These were, at first, modified to become the first Scalextric cars. Because Francis lived near Goodwood racetrack in Sussex, all the accessories for early sets were modelled on the circuit – even the fencing and tiny marshal figures.

It's thought that more than 1600 different models have been made, and almost all of them have wheelbases within half a centimetre of each other so that they're all competitive. The scale has remained constant at 1:32, with a few exceptions. The biggest change in Scalextric occurred in May 1961, when the controls for the cars changed from on/off knobs on a transformer to the trigger controls still familiar today.

The most valuable Scalextric model is the C70 Bugatti Type 59; only

around 100 experimental examples were made in the 1960s, and perfect examples can fetch £3500 today. Unlikely Scalextric models have included a Batmobile, Mutant Ninja Turtles on skateboards, a James Bond set and even racehorses. These are the 10 Scalextric cars most coveted by collectors:

1	C70 Bugatti Type 59	any colour
2	C69 Ferrari 250 GT SWB	in yellow
3	C68 Aston Martin DB4 GT	in yellow
4	24C/101 1:24 scale Jaguar E-type	in red
5	MM/C53 Austin-Healey 100/6, tinplate	any colour
6	CK2 Porsche 904 Carrera GTS	any colour
7	C65 Alfa Romeo 8C 2300	in yellow
8	C71 Auto Union C-type	in yellow
9	24C/500 1:24 scale Lotus 38	any colour
10	C88 Cooper Type 51	in blue

GM's travelling roadshows

General Motors staged its own motor shows intermittently between 1949 and 1961. They became travelling events, touring US cities to promote the corporation's new products and its futuristic ideas in the shape of some amazing concept vehicles. Here's a run-down of each show:

1949 **Title:** *Transportation Unlimited Autorama*
Venues: Boston, New York
Visitors: 591,971
Special exhibits: seven unique Cadillacs

1950 **Title:** *Mid-Century Autorama*
Venue: New York
Visitors: 320,583
Special exhibits: Buick XP 300, Cadillac Debutante

1951 not held, owing to Korean War

1952 not held, owing to Korean War

1953 **Title:** *Motorama*
Venues: Chicago, Miami, New York, Dallas, Kansas, Los Angeles, New York
Visitors: 1,405,143
Special exhibits: Buick Wildcat, Cadillac Le Mans racing car, Cadillac Orleans, Chevrolet Corvette, Oldsmobile Starfire, Pontiac La Parisienne

1954 **Title:** *Motorama*
Venues: Chicago, Miami, Los Angeles, New York, San Francisco
Visitors: 1,926,864
Special exhibits: Buick Wildcat II, Cadillac El Camino, Cadillac La Espada, Cadillac Park Avenue, Chevrolet Nomad, General Motors XP-21, Oldsmobile F88, Pontiac Bonneville Special

1955 **Title:** *Motorama*
Venues: Boston, New York, Miami, Los Angeles, San Francisco
Vistors: 2,237,055
Special exhibits: Buick Wildcat III, Cadillac LaSalle II, Cadillac Eldorado Brougham, Chevrolet Bel Air Nomad

1956 **Title:** *Motorama*
Venues: Boston, Miami, Los Angeles, New York, San Francisco
Vistors: 2,348,231
Special exhibits: Buick Centurion, Cadillac Eldorado Brougham, Cadillac Eldorado Brougham Town Car, General Motors Firebird II, Oldsmobile Golden Rocket, Pontiac Club de Mer

1957 not held

1958 **Title:** *1959 Motorama*
Venues: Boston, New York
Visitors: 606,494
Special exhibits: Cadillac Cyclone, General Motors Firebird III

1959 not held

1960 not held

1961 **Title:** *Motorama*
Venues: Los Angeles, New York, San Francisco
Visitors: 1,026,928
Special exhibits: none

The difference between four-wheel drive and all-wheel drive

The terms 'four-wheel drive' and 'all-wheel drive' mean the same thing, but there is a crucial difference that is widely accepted throughout the car world. Four-wheel drive refers to a manually engaging, part-time system in which the car mostly uses two-wheel drive but can be switched to four, as and when conditions demand. All-wheel drive is a permanently engaged or else automatically engaging four-wheel-drive system: the driver doesn't actually choose the four-wheel-drive mode because the car either supplies it constantly or computer-controlled, sensor-activated equipment turns it on when required. All-wheel drive is far more user-friendly, and almost all conventional passenger cars (including many new small SUVs) now have all-wheel drive where the option of four driven wheels is offered.

Star cuisine in the Michelin Guide

Le Guide Michelin, known by default as the *Michelin Red Guide*, is a handbook that has rated the best restaurants in Europe since 1900. The star ratings it awards, with three stars being the highest, are among the

greatest accolades any chef can hope for, although the idiosyncratic format of the book – and the mystery shrouding the methods of Michelin's fiercely independent inspectors – are a matter of constant debate.

The first guide was published and given away free by French tyremaker Michelin in the earliest days of motoring. It covered all aspects of car travel, including not just food and hotel recommendations but also a directory of garages, petrol stations and even public lavatories. The star system for good cooking was introduced in 1926, with the two- and three-star ratings following in the early 1930s. A price was charged for the book after advertising was dropped.

Today Michelin publishes individual *Red Guides* for France, Austria, the Benelux countries, Italy, Germany, Spain/Portugal, Switzerland, UK/Ireland and the cities of Europe. It recently added New York and San Francisco *Red Guides*, and a Tokyo edition is also planned. One accusation often levelled against the Michelin *Red Guides* is that they are biased towards France and French cuisine. However, Andy Hayler, a food writer, has calculated that Luxembourg, Belgium and Switzerland can all claim more stars per head than France.

These statistics are for 2005, the latest year available, and give the number of one-, two- and three-starred restaurants in each country:

Country	3-star venues	2-star venues	1-star venues	Total stars	Stars per head (% per one million of population)
AUSTRIA	0	4	48	56	6.9
BELGIUM	3	12	79	112	11
DENMARK	0	1	9	11	2.1
FINLAND	0	1	2	4	0.8
FRANCE	26	70	402	620	10.5
GERMANY	6	14	166	212	2.6
GREECE	0	0	3	3	0.3
IRELAND	0	2	1	5	1.4
ITALY	4	23	197	255	4.5
LUXEMBOURG	0	2	10	14	32.6
THE NETHERLANDS	2	7	64	84	5.3
NORWAY	0	1	4	6	1.4
PORTUGAL	0	1	6	8	0.8
SPAIN	4	10	91	123	3.1
SWEDEN	0	1	7	9	1
SWITZERLAND	2	14	80	114	15.7
UK	3	10	201	230	3.9

Where a steering wheel on the 'wrong' side is forbidden

All countries that have signed up to the 1968 Vienna Convention on Road Traffic are obliged to allow the registration of both left- and right-hand-drive vehicles. Therefore, in most countries where road users drive on the right, it is permissible to register to use a left-hand-drive car, and vice versa. In a few, however, going against the flow is prohibited. These are the main examples:

AUSTRALIA	Cars younger than 30 years old with left-hand drive cannot be imported and registered. Exceptions are made in Western Australia and the Northern Territory, where US military bases have been located.
CAMBODIA	Right-hand-drive cars are banned. This is despite the fact that four out of five vehicles on the country's roads are right-hand drive and illegally imported from Thailand.
GAMBIA	Right-hand-drive cars are banned from new local registration.
GHANA	Right-hand-drive cars are banned from new local registration.
NEW ZEALAND	Cars younger than 20 years old with left-hand drive cannot be imported and used; diplomats are exempted.
OMAN	All foreign-registered right-hand-drive cars are banned.
PHILIPPINES	Right-hand-drive cars and vans are banned.
SINGAPORE	Left-hand-drive cars are banned from new local registration; diplomats and temporary tourists are exempted.
SLOVAKIA	Right-hand-drive cars are banned from new local registration.
TAIWAN	Right-hand-drive cars are banned from new local registration. Older right-hand-drive cars already in the country can still be used.
TRINIDAD AND TOBAGO	Left-hand-drive cars are banned, but returning nationals can bring an LHD vehicle back with them; left-hand-drive hearses are allowed.

The 10 greatest motoring attractions around the world

There are hundreds of museums, collections and events around the world devoted to the car. But as motoring spectaculars go, these are the 10 that you should try to see before you die:

1 Henry Ford Museum and the Greenfield Village Dearborn, Michigan, USA
Spectacular tribute to Ford and all he stood for, from his love of the land to his legacy of great cars.

2 Musée Nationale de l'Automobile Mulhouse, France
The famous, Bugatti-rich car collection built up by the Schlumpf brothers in the 1960s and 1970s is now the world's largest automobile museum and an elegant 'mecca' for enthusiasts.

3 Frankfurt Motor Show Germany
Held every two years (odd numbers) for cars, the event is incredible for its vast scale, and the presentation of Germany's next-generation products is always spectacular.

4 Museo Storico Alfa Romeo Milan, Italy
With a heritage like Alfa Romeo's, you'd expect a decent shrine but, still, the factory's own collection is beautifully showcased, touching on everything from grand prix to Gran Luxe.

5 Musée Automobile de la Sarthe Le Mans, France
The purpose-built Le Mans museum opened in 1991 and is a great place to lose yourself in the winners, drama and nostalgia of the world's most famous endurance motor race.

6 Hershey Autojumble Pennsylvania, USA
Held annually in the grounds of the well-known American chocolate-maker; there are 10,000 stalls selling old car stuff and usually 1500 amazing cars on show, too.

7 Essen Motor Show Essen, Germany
Fantastic annual exhibition in Germany devoted to tuning and customizing, always with large displays themed on classic cars and motor sport.

8 Amlux Tokyo, Japan
This incredible downtown architectural landmark is also the world's biggest car showroom, featuring four giant floors stuffed with everything Toyota has to offer.

9 National Motor Museum Beaulieu, Hampshire, UK
From classic to ultra-modern, many of the cars will be familiar, but there are lots and lots of them, as well as motorbikes and eccentricities, and the NMM's unique stately home setting never fails to delight.

10 Mercedes-Benz Museum Stuttgart, Germany
As you'd imagine, there are no half-measures from Mercedes-Benz when it comes to treasuring its past; amazing cars, including all the famous racers, in superb surroundings and futuristic buildings.

The story of the drive-in movies

- The 'Drive-in Theater' was invented, literally, by Richard M. Hollingshead Jr. He applied to the United States Patent and Trademark Office on 6 August 1932 to register his idea, and on 16 May the following year his patent – number 1,909,537 – was granted.

- Hollingshead had refined his concept in the driveway of his home at 212 Thomas Avenue, Camden, New Jersey. He mounted a 1928 Kodak projector on his car's bonnet, pointing at a screen he'd nailed to trees; behind the screen was a radio for sound. His tests included using a lawn sprinkler to simulate rain.

- Hollingshead opened his first Drive-in Theater on a 10-acre (4-ha) site off Wilson Boulevard, Camden, on 6 June 1933. The screen, measuring 40 × 30 feet (12 × 9 m), was erected against a 60 × 130-foot (18 × 40-m) scenario, with sound from RCA-Victor directional speakers. The film was *Wife Beware*, a British comedy.

- There was room for 400 cars. Part of Hollingshead's patent was his system of spacing and angled ramps that allowed every car occupant to get a good view of the screen over the car in front.

- Between 1933 and 1939, 17 more drive-ins opened in (in chronological order): Orefield, Pennsylvania; Galveston, Texas; Los Angeles, California; Weymouth, Massachusetts; Akron, Ohio; Lynn, Massachusetts; Providence, Rhode Island; Miami, Florida; Detroit, Michigan; Cleveland, Ohio; Shrewsbury, Massachusetts; Burbank, California; Methuen, Massachusetts; Long Island, New York; Corpus Christi, Texas; Portland, Maine; and Jacksonville, Florida. By January 1942 there were 95 drive-ins in the United States – with 11 in Ohio alone.

- Drive-in movies saw huge growth in the 1950s: there were 1000 in 1948 but up to 5000 a decade later. Richard Hollingshead, however, did not benefit from this boom because his patent was declared invalid by a Delaware court in May 1950.

• At first, to demonstrate the novel concept, day-time open days were held; bigger drive-ins soon boasted playgrounds for children and a choice of catering for everyone, including a 'car-hop-to-your-seat' service. One large 28-acre (11-ha) venue, the All-Weather Drive-in in Copiague, New York, had an indoor, 1200-seat viewing area and a shuttle train to take customers from their cars to the food concessions.

• The largest drive-in movie theatres are reckoned to be the Troy Drive-in in Detroit, Michigan, and the Panther Drive-in in Lufkin, Texas – each capable of accommodating 3000 cars. The smallest were the Harmony Drive-in, Harmony, Pennsylvania, and the Highway Drive-in, Bamberg, South Carolina, each of which could hold just 50 cars.

• The heyday of the drive-in cinema had passed by the early 1970s. Many lost their family appeal as playgrounds were removed and adult-orientated movies began to be shown. However, despite an estimated 1000 drive-ins lying derelict across the United States today, the theatres have seen a renaissance since the early 1990s, with re-openings, new sites and one Florida venue even expanding to 13 screens.

10 reasons why drivers fail their driving test

The Driving Standards Agency in Britain has compiled this list of common failure points when new drivers sit their test:

1	**Observation at junctions** ineffective observation and judgement	
2	**Reverse parking** ineffective observation or a lack of accuracy	
3	**Use of mirrors** not checking or not acting on the information	
4	**Reversing around a corner** ineffective observation or a lack of accuracy	
5	**Incorrect use of signals** not cancelling or giving misleading signals	
6	**Moving away safely** ineffective observation	
7	**Incorrect positioning on the road** at roundabouts or on bends	
8	**Lack of steering control** steering too early or leaving it too late	
9	**Incorrect positioning to turn right** at junctions and in one-way streets	
10	**Inappropriate speed** travelling too slowly or being hesitant	

The 10 least car-friendly towns and cities

The urban environment is becoming increasingly hostile to the car. In no particular order, these are 10 cities where it is least welcome:

1   Bogotá, Colombia

On Sundays, 70 miles (113 km) of streets in the capital city are closed to cars so that the locals can enjoy playing sport on traffic-free thoroughfares.

2   Fes-al-Bali, Morocco

Reckoned to be the world's biggest car-free conurbation, where 150,000 townsfolk can saunter round the old medina with no risk of being run over.

3   Giethoorn, The Netherlands

A small, little-known town that is off-limits to all vehicles – except boats on the local canal.

4   London, England

The first major capital to introduce congestion charging, in 2003. Hated by many residents and businesses, the scheme has since been expanded.

5   La Rochelle, France

A historic city where much of the picturesque centre is totally car-free; electric cars, however, can roam the streets freely.

6   Nuremberg, Germany

Several square miles of the city's historic downtown district are out of bounds to cars.

7   Segovia, Spain

An ancient city that was protected in the Middle Ages by its stout city walls; these also now happen to mark the boundaries keeping cars out.

8 Stanford University, California, USA

Everyone may need a car in the Golden State, but the campus is open only to pedestrians, cyclists and buses during the day.

9 Växjö, Sweden

A city in the southern part of the Nordic nation, the central area of which is welcoming to pedestrians but very unwelcoming to drivers.

10 Venice, Italy

You can cross the causeway in your car but then it must be left in a multi-storey car park, for this island city has waterways for streets.

Fine-tuning your car sales pitch online

Ben Redford, who has sold thousands of cars on eBay, has these eight tips for anyone thinking of selling their car on the auction website. His general piece of advice is: 'Consider how you'd describe your car to someone you met face-to-face.' These tips are all worth bearing in mind no matter where you eventually sell your car:

1 Highlight all key selling points: low mileage, few owners, any extras, service history, air conditioning.

2 What's special about your vehicle? Does it have any unique or notable features? Recently replaced the battery or brake pads? Include details about why you are selling it.

3 Make sure the write-up is easy to read, with bullet points, colour headings and a simple font.

4 Include plenty of details. These make the buyers more confident and may pre-empt questions from bidders.

5 More pictures mean more bidders, so snap your car inside and out – preferably in good, natural light. Include pictures of your car's documentation.

6 Describe your car honestly. Avoid car-dealer jargon, such as 'mint condition'. Be open about any scrapes or scratches and include pictures of them. Statistics show that a car with a few minor faults, when accurately described, typically sells for more than a car described as flawless.

7 Use some of the listing features of the online auction to draw attention to your car, such as emboldening or highlighting.

8 List your car so that the auction runs over a weekend and ends in the evening, as that is when most people have time to focus on bidding.

The curious death of Cecil Kimber

In 1924 Cecil Kimber founded the MG sports-car marque, becoming, at the age of just 36, the father of the small, affordable sports car. Despite his commercial success, however, Kimber was fired from the parent company in 1941 for accepting a military repair contract without seeking board clearance first. He had little trouble finding another job, and in December 1942 he joined a London engineering company as a super-salesman.

On the night of Sunday, 4 February 1945 (World War II was still raging), Kimber went to King's Cross station in London to catch the 6 pm train bound for Leeds. He intended to alight at Peterborough, one of the first stops, for a sales meeting the following morning. The London and North Eastern Railway's *Silver Fox* locomotive, numbered 2512, rumbled out of the station, hauling its 590-ton, 17-carriage train. However, as heavy rain lashed the rails, *Silver Fox*'s wheels slipped so violently that the engine stalled, and the train began to roll backwards. The route for outgoing trains had already been re-set to allow the 7 pm Aberdeen express to depart from platform 10. But in the King's Cross signal box, a signalman detected what was happening to the stricken Leeds train and tried frantically to divert the by-now runaway train back to platform 15. The last coach had crossed the points before they began to move. The last two coaches derailed and the very last one toppled over.

While 25 injured passengers were ferried to nearby hospitals, rescuers used flame-cutters to reach the final two victims trapped inside. Both were dead. One was Cecil Kirk, a Blackpool fishing-company manager. The other was Cecil Kimber. The severity of the crash meant that train services took 19 days to resume fully. An inspector's report later concluded that brand-new track, barely worn train wheels, the heavy rain and a 1:105 gradient on the line were collectively responsible. Kimber was only on that train because he couldn't get the petrol coupons to drive to Peterborough in his own MG.

Dangerous talk in the car trade

Foreign buyers beware! If you're purchasing a second-hand car in Britain, and especially in the less salubrious parts of London, a good grasp of English is simply not enough. You will need to be familiar with the Cockney rhyming slang and other tricky language that car traders bandy about. Learning these terms and phrases will help buyers avoid being conned:

Cars

birthday a car that's been in stock for a year

camel a car of unusual specification

miler a much-travelled car

monument a car that's proving hard to sell

ringer a stolen car

smoke/smoker a car trader's everyday car

Money

bag/bag of sand £1000 ('a grand')

bullseye £50

George Raft a banker's draft

Gregory a cheque ('Gregory Peck')

gripper £1000

J. Arthur bank (after businessman J. Arthur Rank)

Jeffrey £2000 (after Jeffrey Archer, a novelist who allegedly paid that amount to a prostitute)

monkey £500

pot of tea profit margin

People

Billy Bunter a client or customer ('punter'); often just 'a Billy'

Herbert a dim-witted or gullible customer

Hillman Hunter often just 'a Hillman'; see **Billy Bunter**

knocker a customer who hasn't paid

Pinocchio a client who's being economical with the truth about his car

Rodney see **Herbert**

screamer an irate customer

Technical terms

bog plastic body filler, concealing a crash repair

blow-over a rapid repaint job on a cheap car

drip feed/on the drip payment by instalments

Duke of Kent road tax ('rent')

gobbing see **bog**

haircut an illegal odometer-reading reduction, to hide a car's true mileage

The 10 best, and 10 worst, classic cars to restore

Enthusiasts of old cars are addicted to renovation, but classic models vary enormously in the ease with which they can be made like new. New replacement parts for almost all pre-1945 cars are impossible to find, so reconditioned second-hand or painstakingly handmade reproduction parts have to be used. Although many post-war cars are well served and mechanical components are generally easy to come by, body panels, decorative trim and interior parts are sometimes totally unavailable. Cars with separate chassis and bodies tend to be easier to restore than those with integral construction, and glassfibre bodywork can be rejuvenated far more easily than rusty metal.

If you're contemplating a restoration project of your own, you might find this list of angels and devils helpful before you commit:

The 10 angels

Bristol 406-411 All the tools to make everything you could possibly need await your instructions at Bristol's factory, and the engine's still produced in Canada.

Fairthorpe Electron A crude plastic kit car built using parts widely available in the 1950s; it shouldn't be hard to make even a badly restored one look more than presentable.

Honda S500/S800 Give your local Honda dealer enough notice and he can get anything you need for your Honda S800 through the normal parts channels in Japan. What Honda doesn't have in stock, it will make.

Jaguar E-type The company that made the original bodies can offer you most of a brand-new one even now, and Jaguar mechanical components are plentiful.

Mercedes SL Another car well provided for by the factory that made it. Virtually everything is available just so long as you can stomach the cost. The price of a front bumper alone would buy a perfectly usable family car.

Morris Minor As you read this, new Morris Minor parts are being hammered out in an open-sided 'factory' in Sri Lanka. The number of immaculate cars still running is testimony to this continuity.

Porsche 356 Porsche has its very own 'Historic' division that can supply virtually anything you want for old 356s and 911s. Contrary to what you might have heard, nothing is transferable from the VW Beetle.

Studebaker Avanti Studebaker might be long gone but the Avanti, introduced in 1963, was built until 1992. It's plastic anyway, while the components come from GM, so restoration should be easy.

Talbot Sunbeam Lotus Already a cult car, you'll find the doors will swap from any old Hillman/Chrysler Avenger, and Lotus specialists should have no problem with engine parts. Locating the stick-on silver stripes is the biggest nightmare.

Triumph Herald/Vitesse/Spitfire/GT6 Motoring's answer to Meccano, with removable bodywork, simple chassis and trusty engines. You can, in theory (and with much patience), make them look actually better than new.

The 10 devils

Alfa Romeo Giulietta SS Stunning Bertone silhouette and tantalizing rarity mask a super-complicated structure that rusts easily. Even Alfa connoisseurs blanch at the thought of dismantling one.

Austin Princess IV Not only were there just 200 of these strange, slab-sided saloons – substantially coachbuilt by Vanden Plas in steel and aluminium – but the DS7 engine is a rarity, too.

Borgward Six This was the car that brought the once-noble German firm crashing down, and everything on the rare 2.3-litre car was unique to it, including its all-round pneumatic suspension and four-speed automatic gearbox.

Citroën GS Birotor Production was just rolling when Citroën pulled the plug on its rotary-engined GS. Not only is the engine uncharted water for all but Citroën factory engineers from about 1972, but every body panel – outwardly identical to the normal GS – is different.

Ford Lotus-Cortina MkI On the very first Lotus Cortinas there should be special alloy panels, unique aluminium components, a vastly reworked engine and sundry unique details. All these things are hard and costly to reproduce. *Illustrated below.*

Invicta Black Prince/Jensen PW Only 16 BPs and 19 PWs were made, and no two cars were alike. Both models used an obscure Meadows engine and featured super-heavyweight coachwork. Black Prince has the extra handicap of a primitive CVT gearbox to conquer.

Jaguar MkVII/VIII/IX Beautiful to behold, smashing to drive and satisfying to work on, these big Jags are classics through and through. One problem: they cost as much to restore properly as Bentley Continentals, yet are worth far, far less.

Peugeot 304 cabriolet A very pretty small convertible made during the 1970s, but the body-panel availability is today zero, which is why many surviving examples look so scruffy.

Riley RMC roadster The car with the most intricate bumpers ever, each containing dozens of chrome pieces. Very little of the body is common to other RMs, and you'll still spend as much doing up one as you will on an Aston Martin for, by comparison, an inferior driving experience.

Volkswagen Karmann Ghia 1600 The forgotten Karmann Ghia model has nothing in common, body-wise, with its more familiar and rounded sister car. It is nigh-on impossible to find bits for this model.

The busiest traffic junction in the world

Every day a staggering 706,000 vehicles cross the junction in California where Route 60 meets Diamond Bar. The peak flow is 48,000 vehicles an hour in the rush hour each morning and evening; that's the equivalent of 13 vehicles a second.

The roads really are open on the Isle of Man

There are no speed limits on open roads on the Isle of Man, situated in the Irish Sea between Northern Ireland and the British mainland. Once past a 'National Speed Limit' sign, there are no top speed restrictions. However, there are limits as low as 20 mph (32 km/h) in built-up areas that are strictly monitored, often by police officers with hand-held speed guns. You can also be stopped by police for reckless driving in open country. Between 1993 and 2003, around 10 people were killed annually on the island's roads, and 1042 – often bikers – were seriously injured. In 2004 Man's Department of Transport suggested a 60-mph (97-km/h) speed limit (with a 70-mph/113-km/h maximum on the Mountain Road) in a consultation paper, but dropped the plan after 69 per cent of respondents objected to it.

The origin of lemon

George Akerlof, professor of economics at the University of California, Berkeley, first coined the term 'lemon' to describe a car. In 1970 he wrote a research paper called 'The Market for Lemons: Quality Uncertainty and the Market Mechanism'. This is heavyweight stuff, but put simply it's all about asymmetrical information theory, which concerns the different information available to two parties doing business, depending on whether a party is buying or selling. Akerlof illustrated the point using the second-hand car market. He called good vehicles 'cherries' and dodgy ones 'lemons'. The asymmetrical information relates to the fact that the seller has a much better idea than the buyer about whether the car is a cherry or a lemon.

A potted history of the humble car door

- Cars have had doors ever since the first saloon body styles transferred from horse-drawn carriages in the late 1800s.

- Innovations were few until 1919, when Packard introduced the first wind-up windows to replace leather pull-up straps.

- Until the late 1930s, doors simply hinged off the wood-framed body structure. But with the advent of steel unitary construction, the door apertures/pillars became load-bearing structural components.

- Engineering miscalculations could spell disaster: if all four doors of the 1958 Facel Vega Excellence were opened simultaneously, the car would sag and the doors proved difficult to close again.

- By that time, almost every car had doors hung at their leading edges, replacing the rear-hinged items nicknamed 'suicide doors' because an occupant could leap forwards straight into oncoming traffic.

- Car-door design convention was first challenged by the 'gullwing' doors of the 1954 Mercedes-Benz 300SL. They were centrally hinged along the centre of the roof so they swung upwards; when both were fully open, they resembled the wings of a flying bird.

- Lamborghini's 1971 Countach supercar pioneered scissor-style doors that opened forwards and swung upwards.

- The idea of cargo-carrying doors emerged on the 1930 Burney Streamline, which housed spare wheels in its rear passenger-door cavities. The 1959 Mini introduced door bins to hold maps and sunglasses, and the 1987 Citroën AX offered a door pocket purpose-designed to hold a 2-litre (3½-pint) water bottle. By 1997 Volvo had adapted spare door space to more serious employment by using it to house the first side-impact airbags.

- Hatchback tailgates have been called 'doors' ever since the 'five-door' Renault 16 was revealed in 1965.

- The car door took a leap forward in 2004 when the Peugeot 1007 city car was unveiled. Co-developed with Delphi, the 1007 has doors that open (via an outsize trigger-style handle) by popping out and electronically sliding back to allow access to all four seats (*illustrated below*). Peugeot claims that this is the first door purpose-designed for the neediest driver – the busy urban mum holding children and shopping.

Six things 'they' don't want you to know

The global motor industry wants you, the consumer, to keep buying its products and refrain from asking difficult questions. Here are six issues that carmakers would rather you didn't concern yourself with:

1 Bulk-buying

As a private buyer, you may be able to negotiate a token discount, concession or freebie with your dealer. But you are still subsidizing the massive bargains bigger customers can command. Tristan Young, editor-in-chief of *BusinessCar* magazine, says: 'If you buy in bulk you get a discount – you have better leverage, especially when you get to the bigger

deals of 100-plus vehicles. The prices leasing companies pay, for example, are some of the most tightly guarded secrets in the car industry.' One industry source, who asked not to be named, confirmed that a large European manufacturer recently gave a 40 per cent discount for an order of more than 200 cars and vans. Consider that next to your free second year's servicing.

2 Facelifts

The most costly part of a car to engineer is its central passenger 'cell', which incorporates most of the structural strength. Such elements as the front wings, bonnet and boot lid are bolted on, so it's relatively easy to alter their design, while plastic grilles and bumpers are even cheaper to modify. Popular models share similar, deliberate 'cut lines' between their main structures and these other exterior parts ... so a mid-term refresh can keep sales buoyant. But beware: this is often presented as a brand-new model with much fanfare, when it's usually a cynical ploy to squeeze more sales out of an ageing car.

3 Freedom

Take a good hard look at the next TV car commercial you see, or even an advertising hoarding. Does that car driving along open roads, with not another driver in sight, seem familiar to you? Almost certainly not. Carmakers and their ad agencies will do anything to hide the true nature of everyday motoring, with its traffic jams, speed and parking restrictions, poor road surfaces and careless driving. Claire Beale, editor of advertising-industry weekly *Campaign*, says: 'South Africa is often used for filming. For some deep-seated, psychological reason, getting into the car is a form of escapism for a lot of people. It's a cocoon, and all the imagery is designed to reinforce that. It's all completely unrealistic, of course.'

4 Hybrids

Toyota is well ahead of the game with its hybrid petrol-electric technology. In fact, it has such a lead that rivals have struggled to keep up. For its US-built Escape SUV, Ford has had to swallow its pride and take out licences on Toyota's patents. The problem with this is that it's chokingly expensive. Toyota, already the world's most profitable carmaker, grows richer, while Ford struggles even more. Other manufacturers, such as PSA Peugeot Citroën, must sink huge sums into diesel technology in order to match the hybrid's attractively low emissions and fuel economy. PSA is likely to be first to market a diesel-electric hybrid.

5 Platforms

Like the issue of brand ownership, manufacturers are coy about what is underneath the shiny new metal. In the jargon of a financial analyst, carmakers are proud of their ability to create rolling 'platforms' from which several outwardly different products can be created. This is simple, economies-of-scale stuff, exemplified by Volkswagen's ability to turn the underpinnings of its Golf into an Audi, a Seat or a Skoda. Customers, however, are not quite so pleased to discover that under the skin a premium Jaguar X-type is little different from a proletarian Ford Mondeo, or that a Chrysler 300C is based on an old Mercedes structure.

6 Scrappage

As a 'green' credential, it appears that cars are a good case for recycling because some 75 per cent of a car can be reused. However, they are crushed into cubes. 'This uses a lot of energy', says Blake Lee-Harwood, campaigns director of Greenpeace. 'Cars are impossibly difficult to disassemble.' If you imagine that your old Ford is smelted into your new Ford, then you're probably mistaken. Much scrap metal generated in developed economies is exported, travelling in a decidedly environmentally unsound way halfway around the world to such places as China. 'For as long as steel has had scrap value, scrap merchants have existed', says Lee-Harwood. 'It's nothing to do with the car industry being benign.'

The rationale behind VIN numbers

The Vehicle Identity Number (VIN) is a 17-digit code stamped on every new vehicle. It uses an internationally recognized formula adopted in 1980, and is overseen in Britain by the business services organization BSI. The first three characters of the code are the World Manufacturer Identifier, which indicates the carmaker; characters four to nine identify the car's attributes, including engine and transmission; characters 10 to 17 are the car's individual number. Character 10 denotes the year of build. The system has so far omitted the letters I, O, Q, U and Z, so in Britain a car built in 1980 will have A, a 1981 car B, and so on to a 2000 car with a Y. From then, it's 1 for 2001, 2 for 2002, *etc.*, to 5 for 2005. In 2009, when it runs out of numbers, the system reverts to A.

Should I worry if my car has squeaky brakes?

Noisy brakes – known in the repair trade as 'brake squeal' – are almost always caused by vibration and resonance in such brake parts as the backplate or caliper, or by nearby components in the steering or suspension systems. If something is loose then it will let the world know through squeaking brakes. Quality brake pads have a fabric or rubber dampener fitted to help reduce noise; cheaper ones do not have this, so there is more metal-to-metal contact and thus more chance of noise. Brake squeal, however, does not signify anything dangerous, nor does it affect braking performance. You can get rid of it by applying anti-seize compound to the brake backplate or pad edges, but you'll have to do this regularly to keep them quiet. Taxis tend to squeal more than other vehicles on account of their high mileage and constant stop-start style of driving.

Driving on the left

The world is split between nations where traffic drives either on the left- or the right-hand side of the road. Since the first recorded instance of Zhou-dynasty bureaucrats in China decreeing that men had to use one side of the street and women the other, the flows have gone in different directions for a variety of cultural, empirical and political reasons. The last major change occurred in September 1967, when Sweden switched from driving on the left to the right in order to harmonize with its European neighbours. This is the favoured system for most countries and territories, but the following all drive on the left:

ANGUILLA	ISLE OF MAN	SAINT VINCENT AND
ANTIGUA AND	JAMAICA	THE GRENADINES
BARBUDA	JAPAN	SEYCHELLES
AUSTRALIA	KENYA	SINGAPORE
BAHAMAS	KIRIBATI	SOLOMON ISLANDS
BANGLADESH	LESOTHO	SOUTH AFRICA
BARBADOS	MACAU	SRI LANKA
BERMUDA	MALAWI	SURINAME
BHUTAN	MALAYSIA	SWAZILAND
BOTSWANA	MALDIVES	TANZANIA
BRUNEI	MALTA	THAILAND
CAYMAN ISLANDS	MAURITIUS	TOKELAU
CHANNEL ISLANDS	MONTSERRAT	TONGA
CHRISTMAS ISLAND	MOZAMBIQUE	TRINIDAD AND
COCOS ISLANDS	NAMIBIA	TOBAGO
COOK ISLANDS	NAURU	TURKS AND CAICOS
CYPRUS	NEPAL	ISLANDS
DOMINICA	NEW ZEALAND	TUVALU
EAST TIMOR	NIUE	UGANDA
FALKLAND ISLANDS	NORFOLK ISLAND	UNITED KINGDOM
FIJI	PAKISTAN	VIRGIN ISLANDS
GRENADA	PAPUA NEW GUINEA	ZAMBIA
GUYANA	PITCAIRN ISLANDS	ZIMBABWE
HONG KONG	SAINT HELENA	
INDIA	SAINT KITTS AND	
INDONESIA	NEVIS	
IRELAND	SAINT LUCIA	

A glossary of British and American car terms

The English language has gone separate ways in Britain and the United States, and nowhere is this more evident than in the car world. Here are key terms that sound distinctly odd in the 'other' place:

British	American
Roads	
car park	parking lot
central reservation	median strip
diversion	detour
dual carriageway	divided highway
entry slip road	on ramp
exit slip road	off ramp
flyover	overpass
hairpin bend	switchback
lay-by	pulloff or turnout
level crossing (rail)	grade or railway crossing
motoring	driving
motorist	driver
motorway junction	freeway exit
pavement	sidewalk
pedestrian crossing	crosswalk
petrol station	gas station
restricted area	speed zone
ring road	circular road
road junction	intersection
road surface (to drive on)	pavement
roadworks	construction
roundabout	traffic circle
sliproad	ramp
traffic light	stoplight
traffic-light lens	traffic ball
Vehicles	
accelerator	gas pedal
actuator	servo or switch

aerial	antenna
articulated lorry	semi or tractor-trailer
battery	accumulator
bonnet	hood
boot	trunk
bulkhead	firewall
bumper	fender
car	auto or automobile
car manufacturer	automaker
cubby box	glove box or glove compartment
damper	shock absorber
dipswitch	dimmer switch
dynamo	generator
estate	station wagon
fascia	dashboard
gearbox	transmission
gearlever	stick
handbrake	parking brake
headlights on high beam	brights
hood	convertible top
lorry	truck
manual gearbox	stickshift
number plate	license plate
panda police car	police cruiser
pantechnicon	moving van
petrol	gas or gasoline
quarterlight	vent window
reversing light	back-up light
saloon	sedan
sidelight	parking light
silencer	muffler
sill	rocker panel
tyre	tire
wheel nut	lug nut
windscreen	windshield
wing	fender
wing mirror	sideview mirror

First published 2007 by
Merrell Publishers Limited

Head office
81 Southwark Street
London SE1 0HX

New York office
740 Broadway, Suite 1202
New York, NY 10003

merrellpublishers.com

Text copyright © 2007 Giles Chapman
Illustrations copyright © 2007 the copyright
    holders; see below
Design and layout copyright © 2007
Merrell Publishers Limited

The illustrations in this book have been
reproduced courtesy of Giles Chapman
Library, with the exception of the following:

p.12 Bugatti; p.14 (all) Nicola Bailey;
p. 24 Rolex SA; p. 30 and jacket Ferrari;
p. 34 and jacket Chrysler; p. 37t, c and bc
Nicola Bailey; p. 61 and jacket Aston Martin;
p. 62 Nicola Bailey; p. 65 Bugatti;
p. 67 and jacket Nicola Bailey;
p. 71 Porsche; p. 74 Nicola Bailey;
p. 90 Nicola Bailey; p. 119 fig.1 BMW AG;
p. 141 (all) Nicola Bailey;
p. 147 Peugeot Zephyr Mill courtesy
of Gilberts Food Equipment

The publisher has made every effort to trace
and contact copyright holders of the
illustrations reproduced in this book; it will be
happy to correct in subsequent editions any
errors or omissions that are brought to
its attention.

All rights reserved. No part of this publication
may be reproduced, stored in a retrieval
system or transmitted, in any form or by any
means, electronic, mechanical, photocopying,
recording or otherwise, without the prior
permission in writing from the publisher.

British Library Cataloguing-in-Publication data:
Chapman, Giles
Chapman's car compendium : the essential
book of car facts and trivia
1. Automobiles – Miscellanea
I. Title II. Car compendium
629.2'22'2

ISBN-13: 978-1-8589-4414-2
ISBN-10: 1-8589-4414-7

Produced by Merrell Publishers Limited
Designed by James Alexander at Jade Design
Copy-edited by Yvonne McFarlane
Proof-read by Alan Thatcher

Printed and bound in China